Stop Overthinking

and

Vagus Nerve Stimulation

Life Hacks to End Negative Thinking and Worrying With Proven Tips to Activate Your Vagus Nerve to Manage Anxiety, and Overcome Depression.

(2 Books in 1)

By

Charles P. Carlton

Dr. Lee Henton

Copyright © 2020 – Charles P. Carlton & Dr. Lee Henton

No part of this publication may be reproduced, distributed, or transmitted in any form or by any means, including photocopying, recording, or other electronic or mechanical methods, without the prior written permission of the publisher, except in the case of brief quotations embodied in reviews and certain other non-commercial uses permitted by copyright law.

Disclaimer

This publication is designed to provide reliable information on the subject matter only for educational purposes, and it is not intended to provide medical advice for any medical treatment. You should always consult your doctor or physician for guidance before you stop, start, or alter any prescription medications or attempt to implement the methods discussed. This book is published independently by the author and has no affiliation with any brands or products mentioned within it. The author hereby disclaims any responsibility or liability whatsoever that is incurred from the use or application of the contents of this publication by the purchaser or reader. The purchaser or reader is hereby responsible for his or her own actions.

This 2-in-1 Book Consists of Two Parts:

Part I - How to Stop Overthinking

8 Proven, Practical Techniques to End Anxiety, Stop Negative Thinking, Overcome Worrying, and Live a Healthier, Happier Life.

Part II - The Secrets of Vagus Nerve Stimulation

18 Proven, Science-Backed Exercises and Methods to Activate Your Vagal Tone and Overcome Inflammation, Chronic Stress, Anxiety, Epilepsy, and Depression.

Books By The Same Authors

Books By Charles P. Carlton

How to Stop Overthinking (Change Your Life Series, Book 1)

Cognitive Behavioral Therapy Made Simple (Change Your Life Series, Book 2)

Books By Dr. Lee Henton

The Secrets of Vagus Nerve Stimulation

Vagus Nerve Stimulation and CBT Made Simple

(2 Books in 1)

The 5-Minutes DIY Homemade Hand Sanitizer

The 10-Minutes DIY Homemade Face Mask

Homemade Hand Sanitizer and Homemade Face Mask

(2 Books In 1)

The Budget-Friendly Renal Diet Cookbook

Free Gift

In expression of my gratitude for purchasing my book, I am offering you a free copy of my *Bulletproof Self-Esteem* companion guide, proven to boost your self-confidence in **ONE WEEK**.

To have instant access to this gift, type this link http://bit.ly/346qi8P into your web browser, or you can send an email to charlescarltonpublishing@gmail.com, and I would get your copy across to you.

Table of Contents

Books By The Same Authors 4

About Charles.. 16

About Lee 18

PART I... 19

Introduction 20

Section I – An Introduction to Overthinking and Its Impact on Your Life 24

Chapter 1 25

Let's Get Started 25

    How Our Brain Works When We Overthink?..................... 25

    What Overthinking Is and Isn't?.. 28

    Causes of Overthinking 30

    Signs You Are Being Controlled by Overthinking.............. 31

    Effects of Overthinking on You 34

    Case Study.. 36

    Practice Test 37

Chapter 2 38

Anxiety, Negative Thought and Worry 38

    What Triggers These Feelings? 39

    Write Them Down in a Journal 43

    Why You Should Write Them Down 44

    Case Study 45

    Practice Test 47

Section II – Techniques to Stop Overthinking 50

Chapter 3 51

Reflect on the Bright Side of Life Everyday 51

    You Can't Change the Past or Predict the Future: Live in the Present 51

    Change the Way You Think: Gratitude Vs. Regret 55

    Act with Confidence: Stop Asking "What If"? 57

    Do Away with Negativity and Embrace Positivity 58

    Case Study 59

    Practice Test 60

Chapter 4 65

Create a To-Do List 65
    How Your Life would be Without a To-Do List 66
    How a To-Do List Helps with Overthinking 67
    Maintain a To-Do List & Stick to it 69
    Case Study 76
    Practice Test 77

Chapter 5 79

Live a Minimalist Lifestyle 79
    What is Minimalism? 79
    Benefits of a Minimalist Lifestyle? 80
    How to Apply Minimalism in Your Everyday Life 81
    Case Study 89
    Practice Test 90

Chapter 6 91

Get Rid of the Past and Bad Relationships 91
    Get Unstuck from Your Ugly Memories 91
    How You Can Identify a Bad Relationship 93

    Let Go of Certain People 98

    Tips to Shake Off Bad Relationships from Your Life 100

    Case Study 103

    Practice Test 105

Chapter 7 106

Pursue Your Goals 106

    Discover Your Vocation 107

    What Motivates You? – Your Passions 112

    Note Down Your Life Goals 115

    Connect Goals to Passions and Prioritize Them 116

    Set S.M.A.R.T. Goals 118

    How to Set S.M.A.R.T. Goals that WORKS! 120

    Case Study 123

    Practice Test 124

Chapter 8 126

Practice Mindfulness 126

    What is Mindfulness? 126

    Why You Need to Practice Mindfulness 127

    Effective Techniques for Practicing Mindfulness 129

    Case Study 149

    Practice Test 150

Chapter 9 151

Be Happy 151

    Live Your Best Life: There Is Only One to Live 152

    Steps You Can Take to Be Happy 153

    Case Study 156

    Practice Test 157

Chapter 10 160

Reach Out to Someone 160

    Don't be Afraid to Ask for Help 161

    Talk to a Physician If Everything Else Fails 164

    Case Study 165

    Practice Test 165

Conclusion 167

PART II 171

Introduction 172

Chapter 1 179

Getting to Know Your Vagus Nerve 179

What is the Vagus Nerve? 181

Anatomy of the Vagus Nerve................................. 187

    From the Brainstem Connections 188

    Down to the Neck 190

    Down to the Thorax 195

    Down to the Abdomen 196

Why The Vagus Nerve Is So Important................ 204

    Swallowing of Food 207

    Promotes Digestion.. 208

    Fights Inflammation 212

    Controls Heart Rate and Blood Pressure......... 213

    Facilitates Breathing... 215

    Provides Ear Sensations 216

Manages Hunger and Satiety 216

Gut-Brain Communication 219

Chapter 2 223

Vagal Tone and Why It Matters 223

High Vagal Tone – What it Relates to 225

Low Vagal Tone – What it Relates to 226

Measuring Your Vagal Tone 227

    What is Heart Rate Variability? 228

    Checking Your Heart Rate Variability 230

    Interpreting Your Heart Rate Variability Result 234

Increasing Your Vagal Tone 236

Chapter 3 238

Conditions Associated with The Vagus Nerve 238

    Chronic Stress and Anxiety 239

    Trauma, PTSD, and Depression 242

    Lack of Social Interaction 245

    Sleep Disorders and Disruptive Circadian Rhythm 246

- Chronic Inflammation 248
- Dysfunctional Breathing 251
- Dysfunctional Digestive System 254
- Dysfunctional Heart Rate 256

Chapter 4 260

Substances That May Affect Your Vagus Nerve 260

- Botox 260
- Certain Antibiotics 263
- Heavy Metals 266
- Excess Sugar Intake 269

Chapter 5 273

Stimulating Your Vagus Nerve 273

Natural Exercises and Practices 274

- Deep and Slow Breathing 274
- Humming or Chanting 279
- Singing 280
- Humor Therapy 281

Gargling 282

Gag Reflex 284

Exposure to Cold 285

Sudarshan Kriya Yoga 288

Loving Kindness Meditation 290

Exposure to Sunlight 291

Coffee Enema 293

Massage 296

Movement or Exercise 297

Food and Dietary Supplement 299

Probiotics 299

Omega-3 Fatty Acids 302

Passive Methods of Stimulation 305

Auricular Acupuncture 305

Chiropractor Care 307

Electrical Stimulation 309

Conclusion 315

References 318

About Charles

Charles P. Carlton, a former consultant with a top big 4 global consulting firm, Ernst & Young and a Fortune 100 best companies to work for is a self-help professional, devoted to showing you the tricks on how to hack your life to get the most out of it by getting things done.

His quest for self-discovery led him to retire from the corporate world to fulfill his life-long goals of being a self-help coach and writer.

He specializes in using a cut-through science-based and personal experience approach in connecting with his audience in areas of emotional intelligence, self-esteem, and self-confidence, self-discovery, communication, personal development, and productivity. This has helped him build successful relationships and connections with his audience.

When not writing, Charles loves reading and exploring

the beauty of nature from where most times he gets many thought-provoking inspirations.

About Lee

Dr. Lee Henton is a US-trained General Practice Doctor from the Johns Hopkins University School of Medicine with additional qualification in nutritional medicine from Iowa State University. He is a certified specialist in dietology and nutrition.

He has extensive years of medical and nutritional experience across general medicine, pediatrics, traumatology, addictions, food nutrition, and diet therapy.

He currently runs a co-established private medical and wellness practice where he operates from. His approach is personalized with each client by combining medical and food nutrition counseling. All advice he provides is at par with his experience, as well as with medical and nutritional concepts. He specializes primarily in men and women's health.

He lives in Minnesota with his wife and two daughters.

PART I

How to Stop Overthinking

8 Proven, Practical Techniques to End Anxiety, Stop Negative Thinking, Overcome Worrying, and Live a Healthier, Happier Life.

Introduction

"You only have control over three things in your life – the thoughts you think, the images you visualize, and the actions your take."

— Jack Canfield

This book contains important information, guidelines, and tips on how to prevent and stop you from overthinking and keep your feelings of anxiety, negative thoughts, and worries at bay.

When the stress and demands of modern life get out of hand, people tend to lose their grip over their thoughts and emotions. Many find it hard to rein in their insecurities and doubts about the situation they are currently in. As a result, they fall victim to the analysis paralysis.

At that point, the person feels stuck in a miserable loop of anxious feelings, negative thoughts, and worries. Overcoming this can be quite a difficult feat to achieve—but it is not impossible.

You are more than your thoughts and emotions. You can break free from your past, be more content with living in the moment and be more receptive to the future. You can also do away with certain feelings or things around your home, workplace and relationships that trigger the anxieties, negative thoughts and worries that besiege you. All of these are possible if you make a conscious decision today to take control of your life and change your course for the better.

To accomplish this feat, you need to make significant changes not only in the way you think but also the way you handle your relationships with yourself and the people around you.

This book shall serve as a guide for you to understand better what overthinking is and what it does to different aspects of your life. Reading through the first section of this book shall also help you recognize and identify the sources of your feelings of anxiety, negative thoughts, and worries.

From this point on, you are encouraged to keep a personal journal by your side as you continue reading in order to document your responses to the practice tests in the succeeding chapters of this book. This is critical because you need to see for yourself how the proposed techniques to stop overthinking can be applied to your personal issues.

As attested by multiple studies conducted over the years by mental health experts, the suggested techniques in the second section of this book can help you reduce—if not totally eliminate—the detrimental effects of overthinking and anxiety in various areas of your life.

These techniques can help you:

- improve how you regard your past, present, and future;
- better manage your daily tasks to avoid analysis paralysis;
- eliminate the non-essential things and toxic people in your life;
- improve your chances of achieving your personal goals and finding happiness; and
- get more comfortable about seeking help and of those who care for you, and from those who are qualified to give you the mental health care that you need.

Do not suffer in silence when you have at your fingertips the possible ways out of your current situation. As an author and public speaker, Ken Poirot once emphasized in his book "Mentor Me," "Right now is the best time to create your tomorrow."

Read each chapter carefully, and reflect on how you can apply the points covered to stop overthinking, anxiety, negative thinking, and worrying.

In the words of Zig Ziglar, "People often say that motivation doesn't last. Well, neither does bathing – that's why we recommend it daily."

Hence to stop overthinking using any of the techniques laid out in this book, you have to apply it continuously.

Thanks for downloading this audiobook. I hope you enjoy it!

Section I – An Introduction to Overthinking and Its Impact on Your Life

Chapter 1

Let's Get Started

> "The more you overthink, the less you will understand."
>
> — Habeeb Akande

The path towards a happy and fulfilling life begins with unloading your mind of its unnecessary burdens. Overthinking is considered by many as a natural human behavior. However, this does not mean that you should only accept this without even attempting to counteract its negative effects on the quality of your life.

Before delving deeper into how you can stop yourself from overthinking, you must learn how to recognize the signs that you are engaging in overthinking.

How Our Brain Works When We Overthink?

Overthinking happens when the brain becomes too caught up with certain thoughts, thus causing the person to fail in acting upon the said thoughts. It is essentially a mental state wherein the brain is trapped in a cycle of repeated analysis over the same topic or issue.

As a result, energy is expended unnecessarily, while signs of mental strain begin manifesting in the individual's day-to-day activities and even in one's interactions with other people.

To better demonstrate how the brain works when it is engaged in overthinking, go through the following list of scenarios—some of which may even sound familiar to you:

- You cannot stop thinking about a personal problem or an event that has already transpired. Rather than focus on how to solve your current predicament, you cannot seem to pull yourself away from these thoughts. No matter what you do, your thoughts keep coming back to the problem or the event itself—not what you can do to get yourself out of this situation.

- Something terrible has happened to you. As a result, you cannot seem to stop asking yourself why that has happened to you. You also find yourself ruminating about what would have happened instead if only you had done things a little differently.

- Your mind jumps into the worst conclusions, even without any solid or sound basis at all. It has been occurring to your regularly, so that, by now, the negative thoughts appear to be following some sort of pattern in your head.

- You find yourself obsessing about the tiny details in your day-to-day experiences, especially when it involves interacting with those around you.

- You even come up with dialogues in your head, recreating mentally certain life events where you think you could have done better.

- You assign meaning to every word, thought, and action that sometimes goes beyond what is reasonable and realistic. People also say that you read into things, only to realize later on that they are not worth your time and effort.

If you recognize yourself in any of these scenarios, and if you think that such scenarios happen to you frequently, then you might be falling into the habit of overthinking.

As shown in the examples above, addressing this issue is of the utmost importance. Overthinking is keeping you from moving forward and experiencing new things in life. It is like having your hand-tied with a rope that is attached to a pole. You can only go around in circles around the same thing, over and over again.

What Overthinking Is and Isn't?

Right off the bat, it should be made clear that overthinking is not a form of mental illness. It is, however, a common symptom that can be observed among different types of anxiety disorders.

For example, Ben has been diagnosed with panic disorder. He is prone to overthink about when the next panic attack might happen. If he thinks something might trigger an attack, he cannot help himself but obsess over this possibility. As such, his tendency to overthink these triggers only serves to increase the risk of panic attacks.

You do not have to be suffering from an anxiety disorder to engage in overthinking. This is an all-too-common human experience that happens almost naturally to everyone.

You may feel concerned over what you have said to your friend the last time you talked over the phone. Perhaps, you are worried about an upcoming test or job interview. You might feel a little too conscious about how others perceive you at work. These are just some examples of common scenarios where overthinking is at play.

It should also be noted that there is a distinction between the two forms of overthinking:

- brooding over the past

    Dwelling about the mistakes you have done, and the opportunities you have missed out on can be detrimental to your current happiness and mental state.

- worrying about the future

    The uncertainty of what will happen next can trap a person into a never-ending cycle of "what-ifs" and "should-I's".

Overthinking is also different from introspection. The latter involves gaining personal insights and fresh personal perspectives about a certain matter. You introspect with a clear purpose in mind.

Overthinking, on the other hand, involves negative feelings about things that are usually outside of your control. As such, you will not feel like you have progressed at all after engaging in overthinking.

Causes of Overthinking

There is no single origin or trigger for one to engage in overthinking. It can be born out of genuine worry for one's welfare and those of others. Some overthink as a result of how they have been conditioned to think by their parents, their teachers, and their peers.

Extreme forms of overthinking are believed to be rooted in certain mental and psychological issues that a person is suffering from. These include but are not limited to:

- post-traumatic stress disorder (PTSD);
- panic disorder;
- social anxiety disorder;
- substance-induced anxiety disorder;
- separation anxiety disorder;
- different types of phobias, particularly agoraphobia; and

- physical, mental, and/or emotional trauma.

Linking mental health issues with overthinking, however, is not as straightforward as it may seem. Some experts suggest that overthinking contributes to the decline of one's mental health. However, others are reporting that existing mental health problems can trigger a person to engage in overthinking.

Giving a definitive answer on the actual cause of overthinking, therefore, can get you stuck in a loop. The actual case may also vary from one individual to another.

Rather than ruminate over the exact origin of overthinking, you should focus instead on learning how to assess yourself for signs of overthinking. Through this, you will be able to check if your tendency to overthink is getting out of hand already.

Signs You Are Being Controlled by Overthinking

Much like any human behavior, the effects of overthinking can be described as a dichotomy.

On one end, overthinking may be considered helpful since it allows a person to learn from past experiences and prevent the recurrence of certain mistakes in the future. When used in this way, overthinking can be beneficial in terms of problem solving and decision-making.

The problem begins when these thoughts become excessive, thus creating anxiety, stress, and a sense of fear and dread within the person. At this point, overthinking has gone beyond simply thinking too much about a person or a thing—overthinking has become an obsession that disrupts an individual's capacity to function and interact with other people.

If you are experiencing at least one of the following situations, then it's evident that you are being controlled by overthinking:

- Continually measuring your worth, success, and happiness against the people around you;

- Focusing on the worst possible outcomes whenever you or someone you care for is involved in something risky or dangerous;

- Having trouble in keeping up with and contributing to conversations because you go over your potential responses for too long that either you miss the appropriate timing for your responses, or the conversation itself has already ended;

- Worrying about future activities and task that you must accomplish so much that you feel overwhelmed at just the thought of having to do any of them;

- Repeatedly thinking about personal mistakes and failures from the past, thus preventing you from moving on with your life;

- Repeatedly reliving past trauma, loss, or abusive situation that robs you of your chance to cope with it;

- Failing to calm down your racing thoughts and overwhelming but vague emotions that seemingly manifest out of nowhere.

Please note that the signs of overthinking, as highlighted above, are not exhaustive. However, if you find yourself continuously thinking about certain aspects of your life, or you find yourself in an endless cycle of non-productive thoughts, then that in itself is a sign that you are embroiled in overthinking.

Effects of Overthinking on You

No matter how similar the circumstances are between two people, their respective manner of overthinking would not be the same. As such, the effects of overthinking would be felt differently by each individual.

It has been observed by psychologists, however, that those who cannot control their tendency to overthink suffer from a decreased quality of life. To give you a background on the possible effects of overthinking in your life, here are some common examples of difficulties faced by those who have been identified as chronic over-thinkers:

- Making new friends or keeping the ones they already have can be tough due to their struggles in effectively communicating their thoughts and feelings.

- They find it hard to go out and have fun doing their hobbies because they have already spent their time and energy ruminating about certain matters inside their heads.

- Setting up appointments, or even simply going to the store can be an arduous task for them.

- Taking and exercising full control of their thoughts and emotions seem impossible because their mind is already strained and overworked.

Looking through these points, you can surmise that overthinking can ruin your relationships, isolate you from the rest of the world, and it can increase your risk of developing other serious mental issues, such as depression and anxiety disorder.

The bottom line is that overthinking has wide-reaching effects in almost everything you do and want to do in life. It does not only impose limits on you but also to those who wish to express their support to you. This means that overthinking can create serious problems not only in your personal abilities but also the kind of relationships that you will have.

Currently, there is no single form of treatment that you can adopt to completely relieve yourself of overthinking and its negative effects on you. Perhaps, one day, the mental health community would be able to come up with the ultimate solution for this.

However, this should not stop you from seeking out methods that can help you control your thoughts and eliminate your tendency to overthink. This book shall help you understand and apply the strategies that would work best for you, given the peculiarity of your situation.

Case Study

Amy is a middle-school teacher who frequently found herself worried about what people thought of her as a person, and how people see her worth as a teacher. Whenever she interacted with a parent or a co-teacher, she would usually pause for a second or two to figure out if her words were appropriate or offensive.

At times, Amy would be filled with dread as question upon question began flooding her head. She would attempt to answer all of them, but doing so did not alleviate the stress and discomfort that she felt.

When her overthinking began affecting the quality of her work, Amy decided that it is time to find a way out of the miserable recurring situation. She did not, however, want to settle for a short-term solution.

What Amy wanted was to find a way to stop overthinking for good. She had admitted to herself that something was wrong and that serious steps must be taken as soon as possible. This acknowledgment by itself was a huge step towards her goal.

Practice Test

If you have a similar goal with Amy, you need to take a moment and recognize the effects of overthinking in your life. This will be part of your motivation to pursue your goal to overcome overthinking.

In your personal journal, describe specific incidents in the following key areas of your life where your incessant thoughts have taken over your good sense.

    a. Family

    b. Friendship

    c. Romantic Relationship

    d. Work

    e. Health and Fitness

Then, answer the following questions right after your responses for each area:

- What do you think triggered you to engage in overthinking?
- How did it make you feel at the time?
- How do you feel about that incident now?

Chapter 2

Anxiety, Negative Thought and Worry

"Overthinking can lead to worrying, which leads to anxiety. Anxiety can, at times, be crippling, leave people frozen and unable to act. Overthinking can also lead to depression. Either of these can leave you unable to focus, feeling hopeless, and irritable."

— Brien Blatt

Anxiety is wherein an individual suffers from uncontrollable negative thoughts and excessive feelings of worry. Some people also experience physical symptoms of anxiety, such as chest pains and trembling.

There is no single cause that triggers anxiety, negative thought, or worry. Experts suggest that these feelings originate from the combination of various factors, including genetics and one's external environment.

What is clear at this point is that certain emotions, experiences, and instances can bring out or even worsen the symptoms of anxiety. These factors are referred to as triggers.

What Triggers These Feelings?

Triggers of anxiety, negative thought, and worry vary from one person to another. However, these triggers can be categorized into their probable sources, such as:

- Romantic Relationships

    Relationships are a landmine of potential triggers for anxiety, negative thought, and worry. Even when a couple is just at the start of their relationship, the novelty of being together with another person can put a strain on one's mental and emotional health.

    Having arguments or disagreements with one's partner can be particularly stressful at any point in the relationship. If the couple are not effective communicators, the lack of conflict resolution between them may trigger feelings.

- Family Matters

    You cannot choose your family, so even when they make you feel upset or unhappy, it is nearly impossible to cut them off from your life completely. As a result, spending time with them may cause you to feel elevated anxiety levels and increased negative thoughts.

    Becoming a parent is typically one of the biggest life milestones that a person can have. Even though it is most exciting, the new responsibilities that this entails can be a trigger for many people.

    They may experience doubts about whether or not they will make good parents. Some are also worried about the strain that this will cause to their career, social life, and personal finances.

- Friendships

    Much like your romantic relationships, your friendships may trigger your anxiety, especially when you disagree with your friends. You may also begin harboring negative thoughts about them if you fail to communicate with them effectively. Worrying about the future of your friendship with them would then be a common thing, especially when you begin questioning yourself if you should stay friends with them.

- Jobs and Career

    Your current job and career may cause you to feel these things, especially when you do not enjoy what you are doing. Forcing yourself to work for something that is not your true calling can lead you further into a boring, depressing, and unfulfilled life.

- Money

    Financial worries, such as paying off a debt or having to save up money, are commonly felt by people who suffer from these feelings. Unexpected bills and sudden financial instability have also been identified as strong triggers for many individuals.

- Loss

Loss is often associated with intense feelings of sadness, regret, and fear. An individual who has recently experienced the loss of a loved one may feel anxious about what their life would be from then on. They may also have negative thoughts about the circumstances that have led to the said loss. Some may even feel particularly worried that they will never recover from their grief and that they will never feel normal again.

- Trauma

    Personal traumas, whether they are physical, verbal, or sexual, are particularly harrowing experiences for anyone. They tend to have long-lasting effects, especially when the person cannot help but relieve that specific moment in his/her head over and over again.

- Health Issues

    Receiving an unexpected and/or upsetting diagnosis, especially when it pertains to serious chronic illnesses, can trigger one's anxiety, negative thought, and worry.

Because it is deeply personal, the after-effects of receiving such news are usually intensely felt by the individual.

Many people report having more than one trigger for their anxiety, negative thoughts, and worries. Some experience anxiety attacks with no apparent trigger.

Because of this, you must assess yourself and find out what may trigger these feelings within you. By doing so, you will be able to manage them better later on.

Write Them Down in a Journal

An effective strategy to accurately identify your triggers is to start a journal that is dedicated to recording your experiences and feelings related to anxiety, negative thought, and worry.

You do not have to be a skilled writer to keep a journal. As long as you can communicate your thoughts and feelings in written form, then journaling can be an effective personal management tool for you.

Do not worry about grammar rules or spelling. You do not also have to limit yourself to what is socially acceptable or politically correct. This journal is your personal safe space, where you can reveal your true self.

To guide you through this process, here are some valuable tips that you may apply:

- Look for a place where you can write without being distracted or interrupted.
- Try to write in your journal at least once a day.
- When writing about personal trauma, try focusing on your feelings about the incident rather than the details of the said trauma.
- Give yourself time to reflect upon what you have written down.
- Keep your journal away from prying eyes by storing it somewhere secure.

Why You Should Write Them Down

By writing down your experiences and feelings in a journal, you will be able to:

- give yourself more time to process them later on;

- become more objective when it comes to evaluating and dealing with personal matters;
- increase your tolerance for your anxiety triggers and the various stresses of your daily life;
- transform your negative energy into something more open and creative; and
- gain an insight into how you can move forward from these experiences and feelings.

Feeling anxious, having a negative thought, and being worried are natural parts of being human—as long as they happen to you occasionally. However, experiencing these on a chronic level is a sign that there are deeper issues at play here.

If these feelings are starting to affect the quality of your day-to-day life, then you must learn how to accept the fact that you need help, and that you need to act upon this matter soon.

Case Study

Having decided to work on stopping her tendency to overthink, Amy believed that the best way to start this was to document her journey throughout the entire process. In this way, she would be able to look back at her notes and reflect upon the probable strategies she could take.

Since Amy had already identified and recognized the problem, what she wanted to do at this point was to determine the variables that caused her to overthink. She broke her list down into three: anxiety, negative thinking, and worries. Under each, she added the following sub-categories: family, friends, romantic relationship, work, money, and health.

Over two weeks, Amy wrote down in the journal her personal observations about what triggers her overthinking. She took her time to assign each to their corresponding categories.

When she was done, she looked over her list and found out that most of her triggers were work-related. Of these triggers, three recurring themes had emerged. Her confidence as a teacher could be easily shaken by a comment from a colleague. She felt apprehensive whenever parents would approach her to inquire about the behavior of their children within the classroom. An upcoming performance appraisal on her was also worrying her for some time now.

Following Pareto's 80/20 rule—wherein 80% of her problems would be resolved by working on 20% of her list—Amy was now ready to try out potential solutions to her problem with overthinking.

Practice Test

Refer back to the list you have created during the practice test for the previous chapter. Just like what Amy did, identify the triggers for your anxiety, negative thoughts, and worries that caused you to overthink excessively.

Follow this table format in recording your responses:

	Feelings of Anxiety	**Negative Thoughts**	**Worries**
Romantic Relationship			
Family Matters			
Friendship			

Job & Career

Money

Loss

Trauma

Health

Next, try to highlight the common themes in your responses. To get the most out of your efforts, it is best to stick to resolving a few issues that can potentially cause a bigger impact on the achievement of your goal.

Recurring Theme #1: _____

Recurring Theme #2: _____

Recurring Theme #3: _____

Section II – Techniques to Stop Overthinking

Chapter 3

Reflect on the Bright Side of Life Everyday

"Once you replace negative thoughts with positive ones, you'll start having positive results."

—Willie Nelson

You Can't Change the Past or Predict the Future: Live in the Present

Living in the present can be a difficult feat to achieve for many. Whether it is through their upbringing or as a result of various environmental factors, most people have been conditioned to dwell about the past and to worry about the future. Even today's technology contributes to one's inability to focus on the present.

Take, for example, the notifications you receive from your phone. You may be fully engrossed in whatever you are doing at the moment. Still, when you hear your phone go off, the mind tends to automatically switch to either a past experience or a future event related to the notification you have received.

Other factors that can keep you from staying in the present include:

- the natural tendency of the mind to edit out the positive aspects of your previous experiences, thus making the past seem more negative than it was; and

- the uncertainty of the current situation you are in, which then generates feelings of anxiety, negative thoughts, and worry.

Many people find it difficult to overcome these elements and start living in the present. Some do not even know what it means to be in the present. They cannot imagine how it feels like to be free from their ruminations about the past, and their apprehensions about the future. Most of the time, they simply do not have enough personal will to focus on what is currently happening to them.

Fortunately, there are various ways to get over the challenges of being in the here and now. Through the right mindset and a positive attitude, you can start living in the present and make better life choices.

When you live in acceptance of what has already happened, and what will come to pass, then you will begin seeing things for what they truly are. You will be able to forgive yourself and others for the mistakes that have been made in the past. You will also be able to free yourself from feelings of anxiety and worry about the things that may come your way.

Let me share my personal experience on this subject!

So, it just happens that I had made at some point in my life, quite too many financial mistakes and bad financial investments that did cost me some huge chunk of my savings for the supposed pleasant life I looked forward to living. Not once, not twice, not even thrice. Under these circumstances, I should have typically read the signs on the wall, right? and know what investment is good and bad, but duh! *(laughs)*, I kept sinking in much money in more investments, but this time around, in a bid to recover my previous financial losses. However, I ended up losing more and more. At a point, I lost it and went into bouts of anxiety, negative thoughts, and worries about the mess I created in my finances and how I should have known better after the initial three losses incurred. I would overthink what would become of my financial status, especially at the point of my life where I was somewhat out of a job. I was scared, unhappy, and angry every other day I lived. This feeling went on for as long as I could remember, and then, on one Tuesday morning, I laid woken right on my bed and looked up, gazing into the ceiling before me, and I asked myself, a life-changing question.

"How has my overthinking of the past financial mistakes, what I could have done differently, and what the life I hoped to live in the future has helped me achieve?".

I decided that I was going to leave the past mistakes where it belongs, "the past"— I was going to focus on living in the present by making the most out of it— and that I wasn't going to beat myself up about what the future holds. Consciously deciding on this gave me a great sense of relief and peace.

No matter how much we try, we can't change the past simply because it is out of our control, and no matter how we wish we could predict the future, we simply can't because the universe operates on its terms and conditions. So then, the obvious choice you can make, one which you have control of is to live in the moment and enjoy what each day brings. It sure helps.

Change the Way You Think: Gratitude Vs. Regret

Everyone has felt regret at different points in life. You may have gotten over them by now, but you have

surely experienced how heavy regrets can be.

Regret can be something you have done—whether deliberately or unintentionally—that have hurt yourself or somebody else. You may also feel regret after making a snap decision that resulted in something less favorable than it should have been had you only taken your time.

Having regrets is a normal human experience. Obsessing over them, however, is not healthy nor productive, and would most likely result to overthinking which in turn would produce bouts of anxiety, negative thoughts and worry. There is no way to go back in time and change the circumstances that have led to those regrets. The only way to go is forward.

To overcome a regretful mindset, you must learn how to adapt and apply gratitude in your life. Rather than ruminating about what has happened and what could have been, you should switch your attention to the good things that are happening in your life.

Changing the way you think is not something you can do half-heartedly. You must learn how to practice gratitude whichever way you can. You can do it by literally keeping track of the fortunate instances you have experienced in life. Others find the habit of writing down positive things to help keep them grateful, especially during tough times.

You can even take this further by being thankful for the lessons you have gained from your past, no matter how painful or hard they are. Be thankful that you have managed to live through them, and you have then been given the opportunity to learn from your past mistakes. You are now a step closer to enlightenment and becoming a better version of you.

Once you have chosen to adopt a grateful mindset fully, then you will be able to:

- feel contentment about the blessings in your life;
- gain an optimistic point of view;
- better appreciate the people around you;
- find ways to help those in need; and
- have a higher level of self-awareness.

Take note that successfully overcoming your regrets does not happen overnight. You must be patient with yourself, and continually practice applying gratitude in all aspects of your life. The more you practice it, the easier it becomes to access a grateful mindset, even during trying times.

Act with Confidence: Stop Asking "What If"?

Torturing yourself with the question "what if" gives you nothing but unnecessary feelings of anxiety, negative thoughts, and worry. There is no way to know for sure what will exactly happen by choosing to act in a certain way. It is a waste of time and energy to think about the uncontrollable aspects of the future.

More often than not, obsessing over the possible outcomes of your actions will only make you feel upset. Having no definite answer since there is an endless number of possibilities can be particularly unsettling.

To stop asking yourself this question, you must:

- focus on the here and now of the situation;
- identify the things that are within your control; and

- think of each situation as an opportunity to learn.

If you do end up acting upon the wrong decision, the only healthy thing to do is to learn from it and move on. Do not let your mistake define your present and what your future would become.

Reallocate the time and energy you would have used in overthinking about the what-ifs of the situation into something more productive. Use that as a motivation to make better decisions the next time you are facing a similar circumstance. Remember, you can take more control over your thoughts and actions if you would simply believe you can do so.

Do Away with Negativity and Embrace Positivity

There are days when nothing seems to go your way. The moment you wake up, you just know everything that can go wrong will go wrong.

Since you are already expecting it, any disappointment that comes your way further strengthens the negative vibes that you are feeling. When this happens over and over again, those vibes solidify into a perennial negative mindset.

If this scenario sounds familiar to you, then know that you have the option to turn things around for the better. You are in control, and you can choose how you are going to approach important matters in your life.

From here, you can start nurturing a positive mindset that is centered around your personal growth and development. You can reframe your outlook in life, thus giving you hope and motivation to overcome the challenges that may come your way.

It should be noted that you should actively work on embracing positivity. Once you have acknowledged that you have the right to be happy and that you are ultimately responsible for your happiness, you may then proceed to apply this positive mindset in your day to day life, and the achievement of your goals.

Case Study

While searching for effective strategies to combat the negative effects of overthinking and anxiety, Amy stumbled upon the various research works conducted on the field of positive psychology. There, she learned that she had to let go of what had happened to her in the past to give space to a more positive present and future. She had also realized that her regrets about missed opportunities back in her days at the university were bogging her down.

While writing down these reflections in her journal, Amy decided to apply some of the techniques she had read about. First, she made a list of the blessings and things she feels grateful for in her life. Then, she copied each on a separate sticky note.

Since the most of her triggers were work-related, she posted the said sticky notes on a board beside her work desk. In that way, she could easily see them whenever she needed a boost.

Over a week, she recorded in her journal how she felt after a few minutes of staying at her work desk. She had noted small but steady increments in her mood day by day. There was one positive fluctuation, however, when she took the time to read through some of the posted notes.

Given her observations, Amy resolved to make a habit of counting her blessings and remind herself of what she was thankful for.

Practice Test

Create your gratitude list based on the people, things, and life events that you feel thankful for in different aspects of your life. Follow this suggested format so that you can use this list to answer the following questions.

- Romantic Relationship

    a. _____

    b. _____

    c. _____

    d. _____

    e. _____

- Family

    a. _____

    b. _____

    c. _____

    d. _____

    e. _____

- Friendship

    a. _____

b. _____

c. _____

d. _____

e. _____

- Job & Career

    a. _____

    b. _____

    c. _____

    d. _____

    e. _____

- Money

    a. _____

    b. _____

    c. _____

    d. _____

    e. _____

- Health

    a. _____

    b. _____

    c. _____

    d. _____

    e. _____

- Others

    a. _____

    b. _____

    c. _____

    d. _____

    e. _____

Based on your responses, answer the following questions:

- How do you feel after writing down this list?

- Which category/categories contains the most number of listed items? Describe how you feel about that particular aspect of your life.

- Which category/categories contains the least number of listed items? Describe how you feel about that particular aspect of your life.

- Do you possess a more positive or more negative outlook in life? Why do you think so?

Chapter 4

Create a To-Do List

"Each day, I will accomplish one thing on my to-do list."

— Lailah Gifty Akita

A to-do list is one of the most basic, yet easily overlooked, task management tool at anyone's disposal. Essentially, a to-do list contains information about what you should be doing, how it should be done, and when it must be done.

The principle behind a to-do list is quite simple. It has also been around for so long. However, no matter how simple it is, the problem with a to-do list is that people tend to forget about them eventually.

Some find it too simple that they think it is not effective in serving its purpose. Others recognize the importance and merits of a to-do list, but they lack the discipline in maintaining one in the long run.

To better illustrate to you why you should create and keep a to-do list, the next section covers the effects of having no to-do list in your day-to-day life.

How Your Life would be Without a To-Do List

Life, by nature, is chaotic in itself. This is further complicated by the demands and complexities of the modern way of living.

With the mountain of tasks that you must accomplish day by day, things can quickly become overwhelming. When this builds up, the amount of stress in your life will increase exponentially.

Many experts recommend the usage of a to-do list to manage one's activities and responsibilities better. However, some people find it hard to pick this up as a habit.

Studies show that without a to-do list, an individual's level of productivity significantly drops down. You may also experience the following scenarios when you do not create a to-do list of your own:

- jumping from one task to another, thus decreasing your efficiency in finishing up your tasks;

- missing out on important deadlines because you forgot that you have to do it in the first place;

- being vulnerable to potential distractions around you;

- struggling to achieve a balance between your home life, your work life, and social life, among others;

- having no sense of direction at all especially when it comes to what you should be doing next; and

- lacking the feeling of accomplishment by the end of the day.

To resolve these problems, you should try incorporating the creation of a to-do list in your daily habits.

How a To-Do List Helps with Overthinking

One of the most significant negative effects of overthinking is analysis paralysis. This means that you become stuck in your mind, mulling over the same issue over and over again, without anything to show for it. This then leaves you with little to no time and energy to act and carry out your other tasks.

A to-do list can help you overcome this by keeping you focused and on track with what truly matters. Aside from boosting your productivity, it may also be beneficial to you in psychological terms.

According to researchers, a to-do list can:

- give you the motivation to get things done;
- prevents you from being distracted by your irrelevant thoughts and other unnecessary elements from your environment;
- prevents you from doing unnecessary repetitive behaviors;
- break down complicated tasks that may bring about feelings of anxiety and worry about failing to accomplish the said task;
- improve your pacing, and therefore decrease your stress level;

- relieve you of the pressure to finish everything all at once; and

- relieve you of the worry that you have forgotten to do something important.

Ultimately, a to-do list can also make you feel happy and satisfied. A listing with all the items crossed out serves as proof that your day has been quite productive. You will be able to fight off any feelings of doubt, especially those of self-worth and self-confidence. As such, your mind will have no reason to devolve into an endless spiral of anxiety, negative thoughts, and worry.

Maintain a To-Do List & Stick to it

Many people who do not—and can not—maintain a to-do list view it as a burden. They think of it as a list of chores to do and deadlines to meet. Over time, this perception prevents them from making a habit out of creating and managing a to-do list.

Some people are natural at keeping things organized and on track. However, for those who are not born or conditioned to do so, here are some effective tips that will allow you to maintain and stick to your to-do list:

- Associate your to-do list with positive thoughts and feelings.

  This is the first thing you must do to incorporate a to-do list in your daily life successfully. Remind yourself of the practical benefits of keeping one. Try to recall how good it feels whenever you get to cross something off your list. By doing this, your brain will be conditioned to put things in your to-do list to get it done and crossed off.

- Write the list for the benefit of the future.

  You might not immediately realize the advantages of maintaining a good to-do list, but your future self would appreciate your efforts. No matter how good you are at remembering things, life may throw you a curveball at any moment.

  This may leave you scrambling for direction and information. A to-do list that contains all the important details that you must keep in mind would be a lifeline during those challenging times.

- Categorize the items on your list, depending on their importance and your personal preference.

Many people skip the process of categorizing the items on the to-do list. This is an important step to make because it improves your chances of getting things done. Through this, you would be able to prioritize your tasks better.

One way to categorize your list is by arranging it according to what must be done, and what would be nice to do if you have the extra time. By doing so, you would not miss out on the all-too-important deadlines in your life. It will also remind you of the things you can do with your time, thus saving you from having to rack your head for something to do.

- Accept the fact that to-do lists are changeable.

  Remember, a to-do list is only a tool. Its contents are not rules or demands that you must follow at all costs. Sometimes, you have to change the items in your list to suit your current needs.

  Starting anew is perfectly alright. It shows that you flexible enough to roll with the punches. By learning how to adjust yourself and your to-do list, you will be able to better deal with the stress and anxiety triggers that may come your way.

- Treat your to-do list as a symbol of your accomplishments.

  Conquering your to-do list requires a lot of time and effort. Therefore, it is normal to feel proud about finishing a task in your to-do list.

  Similar to assigning positive feelings to your list, thinking of it as a record of your wins for the day will help you stick to this habit.

  This will also do wonders for your mental health. Anxiety, negative thoughts, and worries will have little to no place left in your head when it is filled with your accomplishments for the day.

Now that you understand the importance of having a to-do list and how maintaining one can drastically simplify any feelings of anxiety, negative thoughts and worries you could have, it is also important to know how to create an effective to-do list.

Creating an Effective To-Do List

Some rush through the process of creating a list, thus giving them a one-word outline that vaguely describes what they must do. As a result, they cannot follow through the listed tasks, which then leaves them an impression that to-do lists simply do not work for them.

To help you write an effective to-do list that WORKS for you, follow these quick and easy steps:

1. **List down three tasks, at most.**

   A shorter list containing the most important tasks that you must accomplish would allow you to get a sense of accomplishment by the end of the day.

2. **Make each task actionable.**

   You can do this by using an active voice rather than simply indicating the outcome that you want to accomplish. For example, instead of listing down "detergent" in your list, you should write "go to the grocery store and buy detergent."

   The first part of the suggested statement may sound obvious and unnecessary to you. However, keep in mind that the more complicated the task, the more helpful it is to include these small details into your to-do list.

3. **Assign the priority level for each task.**

   You may ask yourself which of these tasks would make you feel most accomplished. Your answer would then have to go to the top of your to-do list (priority list) with a "high", "mid", or "low" label depending on their relative urgency to you.

4. **Write down the rest of your tasks in a separate sheet or file (overflow list).**

   They should go to another queue, so that you can focus on what matters. Since the top three tasks are considered as significant items, they may also take up a lot of your time. Therefore, keeping the other tasks in a different list would keep you from feeling overwhelmed.

   Ideally, you should store this where it is accessible but away from your sight. This would enable you to refer to the overflow list when you have run out of things to do in your priority list.

5. **Make your priority to-do list visible.**

   You may transfer them in small post-it notes that you can stick in a location that you frequently see or go to, such as the refrigerator door. If you prefer to add more details, you may opt to use index cards instead.

6. **View each task one at a time.**

   Many people feel overwhelmed whenever they see a list of things that they must do. To prevent this from turning into a negative feeling, you can impose viewing limits upon yourself.

   There are certain task management apps, such as the "Todoist" and "Omnifocus", that allow their users this viewing option. However, if you are using post-it notes or index cards, then you can just simply stack them over one another so that you can only see the topmost item in your list.

7. **Record the status of your task**

   Recording the status of your task whether accomplished or not makes you accountable. It makes you have a deeper reflection on the position of your commitment to fulfilling your tasks for the day. It makes you ponder on how you can improve on your level of accomplishment and also gives you a sense of refocus to ensuring that unaccomplished tasks are executed and taken off your to-do list as quickly as possible.

Case Study

Despite Amy's effort to research about potential strategies, she felt like she was not making much progress on this. Her main problem was that due to the overwhelming amount of information she had amassed, she was not entirely sure where to start. She also kept jumping from one strategy to another, thus leaving her a pile of unfinished tasks.

To resolve this, Amy followed the advice of her best friend, Danny, to make a to-do list. Since this is incredibly personal, she downloaded a task management app on her phone, where she can privately store her to-do list.

Amy also decided to create one list per recurring issue that she had identified earlier. In that way, she would know if she had done any action in resolving the said issues. Using the app, she assigned the priority levels and set up reminders that will notify her now and then of what she should be doing.

After a week of using the to-do list, Amy finally felt like she was back on track with her personal project to stop overthinking.

Practice Test

Create your own to-do list for each day or as required using the format below.

For the "Priority Level", assign each task a "high", "mid", or "low" label depending on their relative urgency to you.

Use the "Status" column the following day to indicate whether or not you have accomplished your tasks.

Task #	Task	Priority Level	Status

Carry out the task listed in the table you have made. On the following day, answer the following questions based on your experience:

- How many tasks have you accomplished?
- How did you feel when you accomplished a task?
- How many tasks have you not accomplished?
- How do you feel now that you have not accomplished a task from yesterday?
- How do you think you can improve upon your level of accomplishment?

Chapter 5

Live a Minimalist Lifestyle

"The secret of happiness, you see, is not found in seeking more, but in developing the capacity to enjoy less."

—Socrates

What is Minimalism?

Many people associate minimalism with stark white walls and sparsely furnished rooms. However, that aspect is only one aspect of minimalism—one that is done out of the personal preference of the individual.

Lifestyle experts consider minimalism as a way of life that encourages intentionality, simplicity, and clarity among its followers. Its applications are not only limited to the home, but also other important aspects of life, such as your relationships, career, and digital presence.

Minimalism promotes the recognition of the value of the things you keep and the people you interact with.

As a result, anything that does not fit with your goals and purpose in life is discarded or avoided.

Some people misunderstand minimalism by equating "less" with "none." However, this assumption does not align with the basic principles of this movement. Minimalists are allowed to keep things with sentimental value—even though the said things do not serve any other function whatsoever. As long as something brings value to your life, then you may choose to keep it with you.

Embracing minimalism may require significant changes in your current lifestyle. It is well worth doing, given the benefits, it brings, especially for the wellness of your mental health.

Benefits of a Minimalist Lifestyle?

A minimalist lifestyle is considered as the complete opposite of a life riddled with anxiety.

Anxiety is characterized by excessive worrying, overthinking, and high levels of stress. As a result, you will lose focus on what you should be doing. You become easily overwhelmed by your responsibilities, negative thoughts, and fears.

This condition is further exacerbated by a cluttered space. It is difficult to relax and be calm in an environment filled with unnecessary and disorganized things.

On the other hand, minimalism promotes a clear focus on the things that matter in life. Therefore, you may be able to pursue your goals and function well without giving in to the distractions around you.

When you adopt a minimalist lifestyle, you will gradually be freed from the rush and demands of the modern way of living. Since you have to disengage from non-value adding activities, you will have more time to pursue the things that you want to do in your life. You may also use this time to improve the quality of relationships that you have with the people around you.

To reap the benefits of a minimalist life, you need to learn how you can incorporate its principles into various aspects of your life. To guide you through this, given below are the essential tips for beginners.

How to Apply Minimalism in Your Everyday Life

- Home

The goal when reducing the clutter in your home is to assess whether or not an item adds value to your home or has a value to you. Based on your assessment, you may categorize each item according to these categories:

- For keeping
- For donation
- For selling
- For disposal

Saving an item may mean that it has practical use in your home, or that it has a sentimental value that makes you want to cherish it. An item may also possess both qualities, like a set of hand towels that you have received as a gift from your mother.

If you choose to donate an item, it is best to select a local organization that helps individuals who may find a use for your item. You may also consider donating them to thrift stores that would sell the item to those in need.

Selling can either be done by holding a garage sale, or by posting it on online platforms.

Through this, you will be able to convert the item into something more useful to you.

Disposing of the items that have no use or no sentimental value to you can be beneficial for your overall wellness. You would typically feel a sense of accomplishment because you have attained your goal for this project. The process itself can also relieve you of stress and anxiety since the items may be contributing to the negative thoughts and feelings that you have.

For this process to be institutionalized within you, it is advisable to make a schedule for this. How frequent you do it depends on your preference. What matters is that you will allot a specific time dedicated to this activity.

- Workplace

    Since your personal space at work is most likely limited only to your workstation, then this is the best starting point. You may begin by removing all items from your desk. Wipe it clean, and remove any stains, if there are any.

    Then, sort through your stuff by assigning their respective value to your work. Anything that does not serve any purpose to your current responsibilities and projects should either be archived somewhere else or discarded properly.

Once you are done, rearrange the things you have identified as essential back on your desk. Dispose of any remaining clutter to keep your workspace clean and organized.

To prevent you from overthinking, which things will be kept and which will be discarded, set a timer to 15 minutes only. By sticking to the time limit, your mind will be forced to focus on your objectives.

You may repeat this process every week, or whenever you notice clutter piling up in your workspace again.

- Relationships (Romantic & Friendship)

By applying minimalism to your relationships, you will be able to finally move on from the painful experiences you have had in the past and replace that emptied space with good memories that you will have with your new relationships.

To do this, you must first let go of the past. Acknowledge the mistakes that you have made and move forward while bringing along only the lessons you have learned from them.

Then, apply the principle of "less is more" in terms of determining the relationships that you want to add and keep in your life. You don't need hundreds of acquaintances when you can have a handful of true friends who have your back no matter what.

- Digital Life

    Digital minimalism aims to ensure that our use of technology is intentional and kept at the barest minimum. It is motivated by the fact that intentionally doing away with digital noise, and optimizing your use of the available digital tools that are important, can tremendously improve the quality of your life.

    In this technologically advanced age, we often get bogged down with lots of digital distractions, which could come in different forms that most times cause us to lose ourselves in the process, leading to an out of control feeling of anxieties, negative thoughts and worries.

To have better control of your thoughts, there are several digital minimalist practices that you can apply to simplify your digital and online presence to gain better control of your thoughts, a few of which I would touch on below.

- Simplifying your Digital Files and Emails

Clutter can also pile up in your files and emails. This can come in various forms, such as an overflowing inbox, or a maxed-out hard drive. Much like physical clutter, these can contribute to your stress level and anxiety.

To apply minimalism to your files and emails, you first have to go through each of your digital files and emails. Delete those that are not important, and categorize those that you will keep. To prevent the mistake of deleting an important file, it is best to save a back-up copy before commencing this activity.

It is easy to put this off for another time, especially since it is not as pressing as your other tasks. However, you have to give time for this, even in small 10-minute bursts throughout the week. By doing this, you will be able to clean up your files and rearrange them in an orderly fashion.

Scheduling this activity regularly would also keep everything manageable for a longer period. A once-a-week backup and cleanup of your digital files and emails should be sufficient enough in most cases.

- Simplifying Usage of Social Media

Social media is a wonderful yet noisy place, which attributes to one of the major sources of anxiety, negative thoughts, and worries. If you fail to use it wisely, you would most likely be caught up with the clutter it freely gives and ending up in rabbit holes. For example, people who visit Facebook regularly may experience a change of mood to somewhat negative because you get caught up comparing your life with others you see on Facebook who appear successful, beautiful, and happy.

Although social media has helped in making useful professional connections easier such as

LinkedIn, even at that, you might feel professional anxiety when your peers are making waves in their careers and life in general. Hence, it has become increasingly important to minimize your usage of social media to keep your mental health in check.

To keep your thoughts in check, you need to realize that most people who put up great posts on social media have a normal life just like you but only put the good stuff they want you to see, leaving out the not so good things about their lives— some people put up a "fake it until you make it" post. The bottom line here is social media isn't real life, and you simply have to take whatever you see on social media with little or better still no interest and go out there in the real world and live your best life.

You can also control what you see on social media. Simply unfriend and unfollow anyone whose posts or feeds are both distracting and of no value to your life. If this still doesn't help, then deactivate your social media accounts and delete the social media app from your phone. Trust me; you'll survive only if you make it an intentional decision. Your mental health comes first before any other thing.

Case Study

One of the potential strategies that Amy was considering is adopting a minimalistic lifestyle. Before trying it out, she decided to analyze first how she could apply it to the key areas in her life. Given that her triggers are work-related, she opted to focus on that during this trial phase.

Booting up her work laptop, Amy looked through her files and inbox to check their current status. She frequently did not take the time to sort her documents into the right folders properly. Most of them are just there on her desktop. Her inbox was also filled with unread messages from the various sites that she had subscribed to while she was conducting her research.

Applying the principles of minimalism, Amy sorted, deleted, and categorized all of her files and emails, over one week. She also unsubscribed from any previously joined mailing list she no longer needed that contributed to the overflow in her inbox. By the end of it, she felt a sense of calm whenever she saw how organized her files and emails are.

To maintain this, she added in her to-do list a regular cleanup of both her files and inbox.

Practice Test

Try to apply the guidelines given earlier in this chapter regarding the reduction of clutter in your digital files. Makes sure to save a backup of your files and emails first before proceeding with this exercise.

After doing this activity, answer the following questions based on your experience:

- How do you feel after completing this exercise?

Do you think you can create a habit out of this? Why or why not?

Chapter 6

Get Rid of the Past and Bad Relationships

"Letting go doesn't mean that you don't care about someone anymore. It's just realizing that the only person you really have control over is yourself."

— Deborah Reber

Get Unstuck from Your Ugly Memories

Letting go of the past is easier said than done. However, people are hardwired to hold on to things that feel familiar and comforting. Even when it is essentially based on a negative experience, the human mind tends to romanticize certain aspects of the past.

Some people use their past as an excuse and basis for the decisions they are making now. For example, Glenn had a nasty argument with his former high school friend, Karen. As a result, he decided to burn bridges between her and his other friends in high school, thinking that he had already outgrown them at this point in his life.

This example shows how dangerous the past can be to your present and future. The kind of memories you keep shapes your current path and controls the direction that you are heading to.

Therefore, if you keep holding on to the past, especially to your negative experiences, then expect misery and loneliness to be your perennial companions in life.

To realign your focus towards a more optimistic and fulfilling future, then you have to learn how to let go of your past. This involves all the mistakes you have made, and the bad decisions that continue to haunt you.

Past relationships are usually riddled with mistakes and bad decisions. Yet, they are often the hardest things to let go of from your past. No matter how badly it ended, people tend to hold on to the experiences and feelings they have had with the former partners.

To free yourself from these memories, you have to take a proactive approach. Time will not simply heal your wounds if you keep prodding at them. You need to actively find ways to sever the ties that keep you from accepting the past and moving on.

Acknowledging the existence of a problem triggers the need for a solution. Therefore, the first step you need to take is recognizing a bad relationship for what it is.

How You Can Identify a Bad Relationship

Many people find it hard to recognize if they are in a bad relationship or not. Some have been conditioned to accept unhealthy expressions of love as normal, while others make up excuses for their partner's flaws. People who feel like they are too deep in their relationship tend to turn a blind on the glaring signs around them.

Some relationship issues can be passed off as mere quirks that you can learn to accept overtime. However, there are serious relationship problems that can make or break a couple.

To help you identify the red flags of a bad relationship, here is a list of the signs that you need to look out for:

- You feel like you have to change yourself to better suit your partner.

  It is perfectly alright to try out new hobbies that your partner has, just to see if you would also enjoy doing them. It is also fine to switch things up in your life, for the benefit of your growth and development as a person.

This becomes a serious issue if you feel like the current version of you would not meet the expectations of your partner. If you find yourself changing the way you normally dress, or if you start changing your opinions and values according to your partner's thoughts and feelings, then your relationship with him/her has crossed the line of what is acceptable and what is not.

- You have to defend your partner to family members and friends.

  Not everyone has to like your partner, but it is alarming when no one among your family and friends like him/her. If they are all uncomfortable with your relationship, then it may be a sign that you have to take a better look at it.

- Your partner frequently criticizes you, even when said criticism had been expressed as a joke.

  By doing this, your partner is putting you down in a passive-aggressive manner. Over time, these criticisms will chip away your self-confidence, which can then lead to feelings of anxiety, negative thoughts, and worries about the future of your relationship with him/her.

- You always find yourself wondering what your partner is doing whenever you are not with him/her.

If your gut is telling you that something is off, then you should first communicate with your partner about your doubts and insecurities. If he/she refuses to engage with you on this, then, more often than not, there is something else going on that could significantly affect your relationship with them.

Tolerating this kind of relationship can be tiresome, especially since it will lead you to overthink things between the two of you.

- Your partner usually makes big decisions for both of you and without consulting you beforehand.

Re-evaluate your relationship if your partner is the only one calling all the shots. It does not have to be as big as buying a house for both of you without consulting you beforehand. Going to events alone that he/she wants to go to reflects the uneven balance of power between the two of you.

- Sometimes, you need to be alone for a moment, but your partner refuses to give you space.

  Self-care is important whether or not you are in a relationship. Wanting some time alone does not mean that you have a problem with your partner. If your partner does not understand that, even after you have explained your reasons to him/her, then your boundaries are being ignored. That is not a good sign because it may develop further into control issues later on.

- You feel responsible for the happiness of your partner.

  If your partner relies on you and only you to be happy, then it can cause an imbalance in your mental and emotional state. For example, your partner blames you whenever he/she is upset or angry. Moreover, he/she expects you to remedy the situation or change yourself to make them feel better.

  Such a situation can put a lot of strain on you mentally and emotionally. Feeling like you have to walk on eggshells around them, just to keep them happy, is a sign that you are in a toxic relationship.

- Your partner controls or at least try to control what you do and who you spend time with.

Many relationship experts consider this as the biggest red flag that you should look out for. If your partner wants to control your finances, your relationships with other people, or even your appearance, then you should take a step back from him/her. Take a serious look at your relationship, and communicate your concerns about his/her control issues over you. How they respond to this would determine whether or not the relationship is worth saving.

- You ask yourself if you are in a bad relationship.

Ignoring the significance of this question can be a source of regret for you later. The simple fact that you are wondering about this is a sign that something is off about your relationship with him/her.

Rather than overthink the answer to this question, it is best to take a more proactive approach. Talk to your partner and see if things can still be changed for the better. If not, then you should get out of that relationship before you get hurt any further.

Though these signs are mainly for romantic relationships, most of these red flags are also applicable to other types of relationships that you have in your life. For instance, having an overly dependent friend can too be taxing for your wellbeing. A controlling family member can be just as toxic as a controlling partner.

Evaluate all the relationships in your life, and see if any of them are leading you to engage in overthinking, or causing you to feel anxiety. Once you have accepted the fact that there is a problem, then it will be easier for you to find the motivation to move on with your life without them.

Let Go of Certain People

Now that you can identify the relationships that are holding you back, you may now start working on how to let go of them. By doing so, you would also leave more space in your life for positive people who share similar interests, values, and outlook in life as you have.

It is highly likely that you have an idea of what kind of relationships you want to have— about the quality of your friends you want or the characteristics you expect of your significant other. Normally, you would avoid people who bring negativity and distractions along with them. If your goal in life is to be happy and free from your worries, then why would you choose to be with someone who makes you feel anxious?

It may sound obvious to you now, but the fact is, many people fail to let go of these types of people in their life. The insecurities that one possesses, as well as the fear of ending up all alone in life, may prevent common sense from taking over. As a result, bad relationships persist, and so do negative thoughts and feelings that one might have.

Be more selective of your relationships since they usually have more influence over your thoughts and actions than you realize. Surround yourself with people who prefer seeing the brighter things in life, rather than those who like to sulk and mope around. Find someone who shares your dreams, so that you can have a worthy companion while you are on your way to attaining them.

Tips to Shake Off Bad Relationships from Your Life

To help you move on from the relationships you have identified as problematic, here are three important tips that you can apply to get rid of the toxic people in your life finally:

- Set and stick to your boundaries.

    Establish clear guidelines on how you will move on and impose them upon yourself. Even if they try to break through the walls you have put up around yourself, keep them up no matter what.

    If you have told yourself that you will stop all forms of communication with them, then do not respond to their texts and calls. Block them from your phone and social media accounts. Do not be tempted to check in on them because you have decided that you are already done with them.

- Stop being overly accommodating to their needs and wants.

    Toxic people will try to take advantage of whatever fondness and concern that you have for them. Being too nice can be detrimental to your progress in moving on from the relationship.

You do not have to be mean to them, however. Just stop trying to make them feel better about the end of your relationship. You are not responsible for their happiness.

- Be firm with your decision.

  Keep in mind that the decision you have made is based on significant reasons to move on from the relationship. If you have trouble remembering them, write them down in your journal. By doing so, you will be able to remind yourself why you need to be firm with your decision, especially when the person you have removed from your life tries to get back in.

  In the case of toxic family members, it can be hard to break off the relationship completely. For such breakups, the best thing you can do is to impose clear limitations on your future interactions with them.

I would share a personal experience on this subject. I once had a colleague when I was still in the business of the 9-5 work-life, who was more of a friend than a colleague. We would get along happily at work. Then all of a sudden, on one fateful regular workday, her attitude toward me changed. It is like she never knew me or we have never met. I made many attempts to figure out what happened or why she was acting so cold around me and indifferent toward me, but all proved to be unsuccessful. I felt it was unfair to be treated so cold, given our friendly history. The thought of bumping into her during work and getting those negative vibes from her sure gave me cold feet, made me anxious, triggered this worry and overthinking loop of what to do or not to do whenever our paths crossed. I felt her opinion of me mattered, and this was taking a toll on my health, my relationship with other colleagues, and, to some extent, on my work. I quickly realized the negative impact of her attitude toward me on my mental state. Then I decided I had had enough of her shenanigans. No more of such was I taking from her, and no more would she cause me to be anxious and worried.

What did I do?

Your guess is as good as my response.

I decided I was going to ignore her attitude toward me, never caring what she thought of me or her opinions about me, stop any further unwarranted communication with her that isn't work-related, and continued living and working like she never existed — literally speaking. That is not to say I disrespected her in any way when doing any of these, but I was simply numb to her presence around me, and sure, this felt good, and I had a great sense of relief from having to be anxious when we bumped into each other.

The bottom line is, the more time you spend away from the people you are trying to get rid of, the better your chances of completely moving on. The time that will be freed up by your breakup can be spent on doing things for yourself or seeking other people who would infuse more positivity into your life.

Let go of those who bring you misery and welcome those who will bring you happiness.

Let's find out how Amy was able to handle a similar situation like mine with her colleagues.

Case Study

Another source of Amy's anxiety is her work colleagues. She was one of the recent additions to the team, so she still had not yet figured out their personalities and work ethics.

Amy's main problem with some of them is the unsolicited comments about her style of teaching and the way she dressed up for work. Due to her anxiety, she had never communicated with them how she felt upon hearing those comments. She was particularly worried that doing so would only alienate her further from them.

Since she had taken up the initiative to stop engaging in overthinking, Amy mustered up the courage to strike up a conversation with Dorothy, one of the teachers who had been pretty vocal about her opinions of her.

During their conversation, Amy realized that the comments were mostly rooted in the generational gap that existed between the two of them. Before ending the conversation, Amy had asked Dorothy to refrain from making comments about her work and her appearance, especially in front of other teachers and students.

Dorothy promised that she would stop, but after two days, Amy had overheard Dorothy talking about her again. This time, her colleague was complaining about the way Amy had confronted her the other day.

Despite feeling hurt, Amy decided to walk away for now. She needed to cool her head down before forming up a plan to resolve this issue.

N.B: To find out how Amy eventually handled the situation with her colleagues, kindly read through to the last chapter.

Practice Test

Based on the points that you have learned in this chapter, answer the following questions about Amy's problem with some of her colleagues:

- Do you think Amy should have confronted Dorothy about the comments on Amy's teaching style and appearance? Why or why not?

- Does Amy's work relationship with Dorothy show any of the warning signs of a bad relationship? Please specify the red flags that you are seeing in their relationship as colleagues.

- If you were in Amy's shoes, how would you treat Dorothy after the recent incident?

Chapter 7

Pursue Your Goals

"I don't focus on what I'm up against. I focus on my goals, and I try to ignore the rest."

—Venus Williams

Pursuing your goals is most often easier said than done. The thought of having to take that big step to change your career path or quitting your job to start and own your own business, write and publish that long-overdue book or books you keep pushing off all in a bid to pursue your goals can be overwhelming, scary and harder to follow through—not necessarily because they are impossible to accomplish, but because they inherently come with an excessive amount of anxieties, negative thoughts, and worries:

- That a million things could go wrong if you embark on this journey.
- That you "may" fail.

- Of what people will think and so on.

It is one thing to set a goal to discontinue the use of certain social media apps on your phone or the internet and fall flat of it, and it is another thing entirely to pursue your life dream only to realize it has been nothing more of a pipe-dream.

Overcoming the feeling of anxieties, negative thoughts, and worries to go after your goals may not be easy, but it is possible, absolutely possible. And I will show you how you can achieve this and be accountable to it in the subsequent paragraphs. One thing is for sure and certain, pursuing your goals vis-à-vis your passions, are one of the most gratifying and fulfilling feelings you could ever wish for. It automatically gives you a heightened sense of purpose, accomplishment, peace, and happiness. You can take this to the bank.

To get started on pursuing your goals, permit me to hold you by your hand as I take the lead (*laughs*).

Discover Your Vocation

Starting in early childhood, parents, teachers, and maybe even friends have asked you this question: what do you want to be when you grow up? Up to your teenage years, plans in life often tend to be vague yet grand. The pressure usually begins to mount during the latter part, when people are about to choose the degree they will pursue in the university, or when they are trying to start a career out of their gained knowledge, talents, and skills.

Therein lies the problem because many people tend to go with what feels okay at the moment. As a result, they switch majors or jobs within the first few couples of years after they have made a decision.

There is nothing wrong with seeking your passions by trying out different things. However, since most people do not yet have a concrete idea of what they want to achieve in life, their decisions to go for a degree or a job are mostly based on what they are trying to avoid—not what they want to do. For instance, they do not want to be stuck in a mundane 9-to-5 job—something like what their fathers and mothers used to do.

That is a shaky foundation for something that you will be doing for around forty years of your life. Having the answer to what you want to be when you grow up is the ideal basis for this kind of decision. However, if that is too hard for you to answer, even now that you are in your adulthood, then perhaps the question that you should be asking yourself is this: what is your vocation?

If you are familiar with the concept of a vocation, here is how it compares to the other two perspectives that one may have about work:

- Job

    A job is a simple means to an end. By doing your job, you will get a paycheck. That paycheck is needed for your day-to-day expenses, for supporting your family, and for paying rent—which is where most of the paycheck typically goes.

    People with jobs look forward to breaks from their work, especially extended ones where they can take a vacation. Even though their jobs are not horrible or completely mundane, whatever they do for work offers little to no life satisfaction at all.

- Career

    People with careers get their satisfaction not from their work itself, but from the possible advancements that they can make by being good at what they do. They are excited about moving up through the ranks, earning a higher salary, and getting better benefits.

As such, careerists do not find it hard to put in extra time to their day-to-day work. They are eager to move up, so they opt to work as hard as they can. However, when the opportunity to move upward is taken away, or when they have nowhere else to go in the field of work they have chosen, then their satisfaction dives down, thus turning their enthusiasm into frustration and disappointment.

- Vocation

    Your calling or vocation refers to the work you do just for its own sake. You will know it is a vocation when you almost feel like you would still happily do the work even if you do not get paid for it. It would make you think that this is exactly what you are meant to do.

    Though vocations have a reputation for being low-paying work, that only holds true during the start. Once you have established yourself and your passion has translated into the quality of work that you do, then you will receive your due, usually many times over. The money and prestige that you can get by finding and applying your vocation, however, are peripheral only to the ultimate benefit that you can get from it.

Your calling allows you to pursue your passions in life in a gratifying way. The work you do makes you feel that you are contributing to a greater good that goes beyond your personal welfare. Furthermore, applying a vocation allows you to make use of special gifts and talents.

Comparing these three, those who work for a job feels the least happiness and satisfaction in life. This is followed by people with a career, while those who have found and followed their calling tend to be the happiest and most satisfied with what they do.

Such an observation is not surprising because a vocation does not only affect your work life. It reflects your true purpose in life. When you find your calling, you will notice the effects in profound ways. Your life will be filled with joy and fulfilment.

People who have not found their vocation yet often find themselves wondering if what they are doing now is what they would want to be doing for the rest of their lives. A great weight will build up in their chest as time goes by.

Discovering your true calling in life is not something that you would usually stumble upon. You may be doing a job that utilizes your talent, but it does fulfil you because the purpose is not related to your passion. You may also be working in a field close to your passions, but the employer does not allow you to make significant contributions using your talent. Neither of these scenarios is ideal for your pursuit of fulfilment from your work.

Therefore, to find your true vocation, you need to recognize not only your skills and talents but also your passions in life.

What Motivates You? – Your Passions

Discovering your passion is not as hard as you think it is. The answer, however, is critical in determining what you want to do in life. This is not limited to those who are just about to enter the university or the workforce. It is also a common problem among those who feel bored, lost, or unfulfilled with their current jobs.

To figure out what truly motivates you, here are some suggestions that you can try out for yourself.

- Answer these three questions.
    - Which topic can you read a thousand books about without getting bored out of your mind?
    - What is the one thing that you do not mind doing for a whole decade without getting paid?
    - How would you spend your time if you are so financially secure that you do not have to work for a living?

    If your answers to these questions have a common theme at the very least, then that is likely your passion in life.

- Visualize your dream job.

    Imagine yourself waking up in the morning even before your alarm has gone off. You dress up quickly, not because you are running late but because you are excited to go to work. The sun is shining brightly outside, and you take a step outside your home. Where are you heading to? What are you about to do when you get to work?

Your passions may be found with the help of your subconscious mind. Let your imagination run free to discover what lies beneath your doubt, worries, and insecurities.

- Recall what you loved doing when you were just a kid.

Did you enjoy drawing pictures or baking cookies with your mom? Do you want to continue doing that now that you are an adult? What are your hobbies that started when you were young and persists to be an interest up to this day? Make these memories as your reference on what you would want to do now.

- Ask your family and close friends for advice.

You do not have to shoulder everything when trying to discover your passions in life. The people who know you best might have some important inputs that can lead you to the right answer.

Do not put them on the spot, however. Let them think about it for some time. This will ensure that what you are getting from them is something worthy of serious consideration.

Note Down Your Life Goals

Now that you have a better idea of what you want to achieve, it is best to write them down in your journal. According to experts, tangibly recording them improves one's odds in transforming them into reality.

The simple act of documenting your goals prompts the subconscious mind to begin thinking of them as opportunities. This is not possible if you are merely thinking of your goals because the brain handles so many things all at once that your goals might be completely overlooked and forgotten.

To start building a habit of noting down your life goals, here is an exercise that you should try doing every morning for the following seven days. In a journal, write down your goals for each important aspect of your life. You can add it to the list below.

- Personal health
- Relationships
- Vocation

Go beyond what you think you can have, or what seems possible at this moment in your life. Instead, write down goals that you want to achieve, regardless of how grand or ambitious it may sound to you right now.

Though this exercise may seem simple, it will enable you to:

- Achieve a higher clarity about your life goals; and
- Recognize the value of opportunities that come your way based on how they would help you achieve your goals.

It is not enough, however, to simply know what you want to do. You also need to gain and sustain the drive to pursue them relentlessly, despite the challenges, anxieties, and worries that you might face along the way. This is how your passions in life can enhance your strategies to achieve your goals.

Connect Goals to Passions and Prioritize Them

You need to make time for your passions since they will lead you to your true purpose in life. To do so, you need to focus on them by centering your goals around your passions in life.

Since you are motivated to pursue what you love, then you would also be more driven to push past the challenges and achieve your goals.

In an ideal world, you will attain whatever you have set your mind to achieve. However, in reality, you can only do so much at a time, no matter how motivated you are. You must, therefore, learn how to prioritize the important life goals that you have on your list.

To do so, here are some guide questions that can help you set your priorities. Answer them truthfully to come up with a list of passion-driven goals that you need to prioritize. It is best to write down your answers in your journal so that you can reflect on them after answering these questions.

- Which of your goals do you think of the most?
- Which of your goals would energize you the most once you have committed to them?

- Which goal would make you feel the proudest once you have accomplished it?

- Which goal would have personal importance to you for the rest of your life?

- Which of your goals is completely aligned with your values?

- Which of your goals is within the bounds of your control and not entirely dependent on your current circumstance or some other person?

Since you have written down your responses, you can review them to gain insight into what your priorities should be. Do not force yourself, though. Take your time. You may even re-do the questions if you are not satisfied with what you can glean off of them.

Once you have assigned priorities to your goals, then you are now ready to proceed in making them more manageable.

Set S.M.A.R.T. Goals

This refers to a goal-setting strategy that translates vaguely written goals into more defined and actionable items. Through this, you would be able to clarify what you should be doing, when you should accomplish it, and how you would know if you have successfully attained them.

The acronym S.M.A.R.T. stands for:

- Specific

  Your goal should be clearly stated so that you would know exactly what you are trying to achieve.

- Measurable

  Through this, you will be able to monitor your progress and stay focused on meeting your projected timeline. As you draw closer to your goal, you would also feel more motivated to push through until the end of the line.

- Achievable

  A goal has to be based on your reality so that you may have a chance to achieve it. However, do not set your goal so low because it will negatively affect your motivation and sense of fulfillment. The sweet spot is somewhere a bit further than your comfort zone. It should stretch you a bit, but not too much that it may strain you.

- Relevant

    This would ensure that the goal you are pursuing is significant to you. Otherwise, you might lose your drive eventually, thus wasting whatever time, effort, and resources that you have already exerted to achieve the said goal.

- Time-Bound

    A goal needs a due date to be effective. Otherwise, you would not be able to impose your priorities well.

How to Set S.M.A.R.T. Goals that WORKS!

To help you effectively apply the principles of S.M.A.R.T. to your goals, here are some essential questions you should answer.

- Specific

    You may define your goal in great detail by answering the 5 "W" questions:

    - What do you want to achieve?
    - Why is this goal significant to you?

- Who are the people involved in achieving this goal?
- Where is it going to take place?
- Which of your resources and limitations would apply to this goal?

- Measurable

    You may assess the measurability of your goal if it addresses the following questions:

    - How many/much _____ do you need to achieve your goal?
    - How will you know if you have already achieved your goal?

- Achievable

    To make your goal attainable, answer the following guide questions:

    - What strategy/strategies are you going to use to accomplish your goal?
    - How realistic is your goal against your current personal limitations (i.e., skills, talents, financial status, etc.)?

- Relevant

    A goal is relevant to you if you can answer "yes" to the following questions:

    - Is the goal worth your time, effort, and resources?
    - Is it the right time to pursue this goal?
    - Is it aligned with your other goals and needs in life?

- Time-Bound

    You can establish the timeline for your goal by answering these questions:

    - When do you need to accomplish this goal?
    - What can you do today/___ week from now/___ month from now/___ year from now to get closer to your goal?

To make your S.M.A.R.T. goals even more effective, you should positively construct them. For example, rather than saying, "Do not skip breakfast," you should say, "Eat a healthy and balanced meal during breakfast time every day."

You should also reflect upon your list of S.M.A.R.T. goals regularly. Set a schedule for your reviews and personal evaluations. This will help you keep your list up-to-date vis-à-vis your current situation and what you have achieved so far.

If you have diligently followed through with this very chapter, I believe you should have been able to gain an enormous amount of inner strength and insights that have not only helped you to discover your vocation (if you haven't before now) but to also help you in pursuing your goals to the finish line without having to feel any form of anxiety, negative thought or worry of not pulling through.

Case Study

Aside from making to-do lists, Amy had also decided to set effective goals that will ultimately lead her to stop overthinking on how to go about pursuing and achieving her goals. To do this, she applied the principles of S.M.A.R.T. goals.

Using her list of recurring triggers as her basis, Amy formed goals for the successful resolution of each trigger. For example, under the trigger prompted by her upcoming performance appraisal, she wrote down this goal:

"At least one week before the performance appraisal, conduct a dry run of the proposed lesson plan to be used for the evaluation with a different set of students."

Practice Test

Analyze Amy's sub-goal to ace the performance appraisal vis-à-vis the elements of S.M.A.R.T. goal-setting strategy. Evaluate how well Amy had implemented these principles of this strategy. Indicate the good points and the points for improvement for each element. You may use the guide questions above as a point of reference in your evaluation when setting your goals.

- Specific?

  _____
  _____
  _____
  _____

- Measurable?

_____
_____
_____
_____

- Achievable?

_____
_____
_____
_____

- Realistic?

_____
_____
_____
_____

- Time-Bound?

_____
_____
_____
_____

Chapter 8

Practice Mindfulness

"Remember then: there is only one important time—now! It is the most important time because it is the only time when we have any power."

—Leo Tolstoy

What is Mindfulness?

When your mind is fully focused on what is currently happening to you, on what you are doing, and on the environment where you live in, you are experiencing the phenomenon called mindfulness.

It might seem like something that anyone can do naturally. After all, everyone possesses the potential to achieve this quality through practice.

However, the human mind is prone to wandering. At that point, you will lose touch with what your body is feeling and going through. If this goes on further, obsessive and intrusive thoughts will begin invading your mind, filling it with negative thoughts and worries about the future. In time, this can lead to full, blown anxiety.

Fortunately, no matter how far your mind has gone, mindfulness can bring you back to the present, where you can be, once again, completely aware of your actions and feelings.

Why You Need to Practice Mindfulness

Practicing mindfulness allows you to have better access to its benefits. According to experts, mindfulness can:

- Reduce your level of stress;
- Enable you to gain insight about your inner self;
- Improve your self-awareness, particularly about your thoughts;
- Enhance your physical and mental performance;
- Make you feel happier;
- Increase your level of patience;
- Make you more accepting of the changes in your life; and

- Lower down your feelings of frustration and disappointment.

Mindfulness also fosters your ability to see things from the perspective of others. Through this, you may be able to relieve yourself of your negative thoughts and worries about how others think or feel about you.

For example, your friend snapped at you when you had asked her about her day. At first, you might worry about whether or not you have done something to upset her.

However, if you could set aside this automatic response for even a moment, then you might be able to recall that she mentioned something about having a hard time finishing up a paper. You could then surmise that her foul mood may have resulted from being stressed out by her deadline.

This alternative explanation of your friend's behavior may help alleviate your earlier worries about your actions towards her. You would also feel less bad about being unintentionally snapped at by your friend.

Effective Techniques for Practicing Mindfulness

Even though mindfulness is an innate human ability, you can still improve your access to it by applying various techniques, such as:

- Mindful Meditation

    This technique works best if you would do it in a quiet spot that is free from clutter. It should be well ventilated and well lighted, ideally by natural light.

    Once you have found the perfect spot for this, you must follow these steps to perform mindful meditation properly:

    o Take a seat.

    It can be a chair, a bench, or a floor cushion, as long as it is stable and comfortable.

    o Adjust the position of your legs.

    If you are sitting on a chair or a bench, it is best to keep both feet on the ground. If you are sitting down on the floor, then you should cross both your legs in front of you.

- o Adopt a straight posture for your upper body.

  Do not overdo it by straining your spine out of its natural curvature. The angle of your head and shoulders must feel comfortable to prevent their positions from being a source of distraction for you later on.

- o Place your upper arms in a parallel position to your upper body.

- o Gently place your hands on top of your legs.

  Maintain the positioning of your upper arms from the previous step. This will keep you from either slouching forward or leaning too far back.

- o Slowly drop your gaze along with your chin.

  You may also lower your upper lid, or even close them if it would make you feel more comfortable. Take note, however, that this is not necessary for mindful meditation.

- o Relax, and be there at the moment.

    Observe if you would feel any unusual sensations in your body.

- o Feel and follow your breathing.

    Take note of the air flowing in through your nose or mouth. Observe how your chest or stomach rise and fall with each breath you take.

- o When other thoughts enter your mind, do not block them.

    Instead, just gently realign your focus on your breathing once you have noticed that you have drifted away.

- o If you need to move your body, take a quick pause before acting upon it.

    There are times when you have to move a body part to feel more comfortable. Sometimes, you would also feel an itch that you just have to scratch. You are allowed to move your body as long as the movement is deliberate and intentional on your part. The pause that you will take before each movement would enable you to make this transition a success.

o When you feel relaxed yet focused, you may lift your gaze and chin once more.

If you had closed your eyes, then you may now open them. Once you do, take note of how your body feels during that moment. Notice the first thoughts and emotions that will rise to the surface as well.

Based on what you have noted, decide on how you should proceed with the rest of your day.

In case you want to incorporate music into your mindful meditation session, then you can try using the iOS and Android app called "Relax Melodies." Unlike most other meditation apps that include guided meditation tracks, this one only contains background music that you can use while meditating. Therefore, this is an excellent option for those who already have experience in mindful meditation but want to enhance their experience further. Since this app is for free, feel free to try it and see if it would be of any use to you.

- Mindful Observation

    Through this exercise, you will be able to gain a better and deeper appreciation of even the simplest elements in your current environment. Thus, you will feel a connection with the natural beauty of the things around you—something that would not have been possible because you always seem to be in a rush to go somewhere else.

    To do this, you must:

    - Choose a natural object that can be found within your field of sight.

        This can be a plant, the clouds in the sky, or even an insect.

    - Focus and observe it for a minute or two.

        Do not engage in anything else while you are doing this. Try to relax your body and mind as you do so.

- Look at the object with awe and wonderment, as if this is the first time that you see it.

- Explore with your eyes the form of the object.

  Let your attention be consumed by its mere presence.

- Allow yourself to connect with the object in terms of its role in the natural world, and based on the general vibes that you are getting from it.

- Mindful Listening

This technique involves the presence of two elements: attention and intention. If you can stay in the present, and remain open and unbiased no matter what you hear, then you have the element of focus.

On the other hand, the element of intention is present when you possess a genuine interest in what the other person is saying.

Mindful listening, however, is not simply listening well to others. It also pertains to an individual's ability to listen well to himself/herself. If you are not aware of your personal beliefs, needs, aspirations, and fears, then you will not have much capacity to listen to somebody else's.

To help you apply this technique, here are some essential tips about mindful listening:

- Check inward first.

  If you are feeling something off or unpleasant, then you have to address that first before engaging with others.

- Get a feel of your own presence.

  Let the other person feel your interest and feelings of empathy, too.

- Take note in the silence of any reactions you might have.

  Quickly note your reactions as they arise, and then return your attention to the speaker.

- Make the other person feel heard.

> You may do this by reflecting upon the speaker's words and saying back a summary of his/her main points.

- o Keep things going by using open-ended questions.

> You may ask questions to clarify points that you do not understand and to probe for more information.

- Mindful Breathing

You may practice this in whatever position is most comfortable for you. Keeping your eyes open or closed also depends on which one would make you concentrate more.

As a guide, here is a short step-by-step process on how to do mindful breathing:

- o Assume a comfortable position that will relax your body.

- o Pay attention to the shape of your body and the sensations that you can feel across different body parts.

- o Switch your focus to your breathing.

- Feel the natural flow of air in and out of your body.
- Take note of the sensations in between each breath.
- If your mind starts drifting off to other topics while doing this exercise, acknowledge first that you are straying off from the path by whispering under your breath "wondering" or "thinking." Then, gently realign your focus back to your breathing.
- After around 5 minutes, switch your attention back to the rest of your body.
- Feel how more relaxed you are now.
- Proceed with the rest of your day more mindfully.

- Mindful Walking

This technique is particularly useful because you will walk at some point during the day. You can better utilize that time spent walking by engaging your body and mind with a mindful and meditative exercise.

To guide you through this here is one form of mindful walking that you can do even while walking down a street:

- Assume a straight posture.
- Curl in the thumb of your left hand, and then close the rest of your fingers over it.
- Place your left hand in the spot above your belly button.
- Place your right hand over your left hand, resting the right thumb in the space between the left thumb and the left index finger.
- Slightly drop your gaze.
- Take your first step using your left foot.
- Take another step using your right foot.
- Follow a steady, mindful pace.
- If your mind wanders off, bring it back by focusing again on the sensations of your feet as they touch the ground.

- Guided Meditation

If you do not know where and how to start meditating properly, you may consider trying guided meditations. Through this, you will be able to practice conjuring up mental imageries as you meditate or incorporate different breathing exercises into your routine. Others also teach you how to create personal mantras that you can use for meditation.

There are various sources of guided meditations, including:

- Apps

    Go through the app store on your phone or tablet to find one that would suit your needs. Take note, however, that the popularity of the app does not indicate its quality. Read through the description, and if possible, reviews from actual users to get a better sense of what you may expect from the app.

    Here are some of the suggested apps geared for beginners:

    a. "Mindfulness Training"

You can get the first two lessons for free in the iOS app store. From these two lessons, you will be able to get 6 sample guided meditations that you can try out for yourself.

b. "Headspace"

This app may be downloaded for both iOS and Android devices. Its main purpose is to be your personal trainer when it comes to your daily meditation practice. You can get this out for free for the first ten days. After that, you will have the option to proceed by subscribing to it for a month, a year, or even a lifetime.

c. "Simply Being"

Through this app, you may be able to customize your meditation experience. You can set your preferred duration for each session, as well as the sounds that you can hear to make the session more immersive. You may choose from nature sounds, guiding voices, music, or a combination of any of these three. This is available on the iOS and Android platforms for $1.99.

- Podcasts

    There are various podcasts available nowadays on the topic of meditation, as well as quick guided meditation practices that you can use to learn the ropes in your own time. Here a few suggested podcasts you can try out based on their popularity. A simple search of these on Google would direct you to where you can listen to these podcasts.

    a. The daily meditation podcast with Mary Meckley

    b. 10% happier with Dan Harris

    c. Tara Brach

    d. The meditation Oasis

    e. Meditation Minis

- Reflect on Your Thoughts

  The objective of this mindfulness exercise is to establish a deeper connection with your thoughts. Here are some tips that you can do to practice this:

    o You can start this by asking yourself first about the things that you are grateful for.

    o To prevent the logical part of your brain from answering, experts suggest referring to yourself in the second person.

      As such, the correct form of a possible starting question is, "What are you feeling most grateful for right now?"

    o Thoughts related to this question would surely come to the forefront of your mind.

    o Stay connected to the natural flow of your thoughts.

      Avoid trying to direct it in a different direction.

- Form a deep connection with your thoughts as you continue paying your complete attention to them.

To keep yourself from being immersed in this activity for too long, you may use an app, such as the "Insight Timer," to preset a duration for each session. The benefit of using apps like this is that its method of notifying you is significantly less jarring than the alarm timer on your phone. As a result, you will be able to retain the mindful state that you have entered, even after the session has ended.

- Self-Compassion Break

    This technique serves as a personal reminder to apply mindfulness, kindness, and common humanity—the three core components of self-compassion—whenever you are facing difficulties in your life.

    For this method to be effective, you have to make use of the soothing properties of human touch. You must also find a way to communicate with yourself effectively. It will only distract you if you cannot agree with yourself about the meaning of your words.

Here is a step-by-step process on how to conduct a self-compassion break. Ideally, you should be doing this with your eyes closed to focus more on your inner self.

- o Think of a personal life situation that is making you feel stressed out.

    This may be a health issue, problems with your partner or family member, financial difficulties, or work struggles.

- o Select a specific problem within that aspect.

    It should not be that big of a problem. You have just started doing this, so it is best to stick to the mild to moderate range for now.

- o Visualize your chosen situation.

    Picture in your mind the setting of the situation. If there is dialogue involved, identify the speakers and who is saying what to whom. Go into the details of what is happening and what might happen.

- Take note of the sensations in your body.

    Are you feeling any sort of discomfort while you are visualizing the situation in your mind? If you do not, then you should go back to step 2 and choose a slightly more stressful problem.

- When you feel discomfort in your body, recognize it for what it is.

    You may try saying the following statements, whichever sounds right to you. By doing this, you are exhibiting mindfulness.

    a. "This is a moment of suffering."

    b. "This moment is painful for me."

    c. "This is so stressful."

- To channel your common humanity, acknowledge that struggle is part of the normal human experience.

    You may do so by saying out loud any of these statements:

    a. "Suffering is a part of being human."

- b. "I am not alone. Everyone suffers at some point in their lives."
- c. "Other people feel this kind of pain, too when they are struggling."

o Offer yourself a gesture that would soothe yourself, along with a message of kindness to yourself.

This may be expressed through the following sample statements:

- a. "May I accept myself as I am."
- b. "May I be kind to myself."
- c. "May I be patient. May I be strong."
- d. "May I provide for myself whatever I need."

If you cannot think of the right words to say to yourself, then imagine offering support to a family member or a close friend who is suffering from a similar problem as you. What are the words that you will choose then? How can you deliver your message of kindness to those you care about?

Think about this, and see if you can offer the same kind of treatment and support to yourself.

- Body Scan

  Through similar principles of meditation, this technique can enable you to establish a deep connection with your body. As the name implies, it involves a conscious scanning of your body, from the top of your head to the tip of your toes.

  During the process, you will become hyper-aware of any unusual sensations, discomfort, and pains within your body. These are crucial pieces of information because, depending on their location, these may be indicators of an anxious mind and a worn-out body.

  To apply this technique, allocate at least 30 minutes for this activity. It is also best to lie down on a mat or a bed, but you may also do this in a sitting position. Choose whichever position would allow you to stay awake and alert throughout the following activity.

  - Close your eyes.

This will help you keep your focus on what matters. If you are not comfortable with this, you may just half-close your eyes.

- Take note of your breathing and your point of contact with the surface you are lying on or sitting on.

  Take as much time as you need to examine the movement and specified areas of your body.

- Once you are ready, take a deep breath before moving on to the examination of another body part.

  You can either follow a system wherein you examine everything from your head down to your toes, or you may choose which areas to observe randomly.

- Take note of any sensation you are currently feeling in the body part you are examining.

  These sensations include, but are not limited to, tightness, tingling, high or low temperature, pressure, or buzzing. If you cannot feel anything, then that is perfectly fine. Take note of that too.

Your objective for this step is to simply notice your current feelings and sensations. Do not judge anything yet at this point.

- After you have explored the sensations from different parts of your body, expand the scope of your attention to your whole body.

Spend a few minutes just breathing in and out freely as you get an overall feel of your bodily sensations.

- You may now proceed with the rest of your day.

Make your movements more deliberate than usual to retain your current mental state for a longer period.

Case Study

Another strategy that Amy had taken up was practicing mindfulness. Since she was a beginner, she selected guided meditations as her preferred method. She downloaded an app on her phone and set a schedule for her session.

Though she found it hard to achieve a mindful state during her first try, she did notice that she felt more relaxed and calmer after the activity. Because of this, she decided to include this in her weekly to-do list.

Practice Test

Download at least one of the suggested apps for guided meditation given earlier in this chapter. Just like Amy, try out a session, and then answer the following questions based on your experience:

- How do you feel after doing this activity?

- Do you think you have met your goal for this activity? Why or why not?

- Would you try doing this again until it becomes one of your habits? Why or why not?

Chapter 9

Be Happy

> If we would just slow down, happiness would catch up to us.
>
> — Richard Carlson

As confirmed by multiple studies, happiness is crucial to one's overall mental health. Happy people tend to have better relationships with the people around them. They find it easier to pursue their true passions in life, and therefore find success in what they have chosen to do. Their happiness also protects them from harmful elements that could lower down the quality of their life, such as overthinking and anxiety.

Attaining happiness in your life is not an easy feat to achieve. Some people assume that there are special techniques that will make them happy overnight. However, that is what makes happiness elusive to them.

Rather than a destination that you need to go to, happiness is found in the journey itself. It is a way of life that makes you feel fulfilled and contented. No matter what your status in life is, you can find happiness with the people around you and in the things that you do.

Live Your Best Life: There Is Only One to Live

You need to make the most out of the life you currently have by finding happiness, purpose, and satisfaction in your life.

A lot of people tend to forget that they have a choice on how to live their lives. They let themselves be stuck in their miserable situations, complaining and whining about how unfair everything is around them.

It is natural for humans to dream for the best possible future for them. However, this can only go so far if that is the only thing that you will do. You have to take action and live your life in the best possible way. This goes beyond simple wishful thinking. It involves finding your true purpose in life and pursuing your passions.

Living up to your full potential is only one way to go about this, though. You can also aim to live a well-balanced life. By figuring out the right balance in the key areas of your life, you would be able to go after the things that will make you happy and fulfilled.

To live your best life, you must commit to creating this kind of life for yourself. You have to commit to facing the challenges of personal growth and development. Only then can you have the strength, courage, and determination to live your best life.

Steps You Can Take to Be Happy

You are in charge of finding your happiness. To guide you through this, here are some actionable steps that you can take right now:

- Add more foods that are rich in tyrosine into your diet.

    Tyrosine is an amino acid that increases the production of dopamine—or also known as the feel-good hormone—in your brain. Excellent sources of tyrosine include almonds, avocados, bananas, and eggs.

- Practice relaxation exercises regularly.

    You may go for a nice massage or a long walk in the park. Meditation has also been proven to be an effective way of calming both the body and the mind.

- Get enough high-quality sleep.

   This means that upon waking up, you feel well-rested and more energized. To achieve this, some people set a regular sleeping schedule that enables the REM cycle to complete its course. Others design a sleeping ritual that would put the body and mind into the optimal sleeping condition.

- Make your fitness a priority.

   Exercising regularly increases the dopamine levels in your brain. You do not have to get a gym subscription for this to be effective. You can go for simple activities such as power walking, running, lifting weights, or swimming.

- Practice mindfulness.

   Pay complete attention to everything you do. Avoid giving in to distractions and immerse yourself with the moment. You can practice this by adopting any of your preferred mindfulness techniques elucidated in the previous chapter.

- Be grateful

    Keep track of the things that you feel thankful for.

    This may be the people you cherish in your life, or the places you frequent to, or the work projects that you are currently enjoying. For better results, record them in a journal. By doing so, you will be able to refer to them as well whenever you need a little boost.

- Stop comparing yourself with others.

    There is no point comparing yourself with other people because everyone is likely at different phases in their lives. Comparing yourself against someone who is more established in life would only make you miserable.

- Work for meaningful goals, not money.

    You will be more fulfilled if your work is aligned with your purpose in life. No matter how demanding it is, or how little you get paid for doing it, pursuing your vocation would significantly increase your chances of finding happiness.

- Spend more time with positive people.

One of the basic human needs is socializing. However, it is not just simply the amount of time you spend but also the quality of the time you spend with them. This means that you have to engage in constructive and uplifting activities to generate happiness within you.

The personalities and interests of the people you associate with also factors into your happiness. Ideally, you should select positive-thinking individuals who share similar values as you do.

- Keep good memories, and let go of the bad ones.

   Your memories are your constant companions. Therefore, they can influence your mood and outlook in life in significant ways. Cherish the good memories you have so that you will have a source of inspiration and motivation, especially in times of need.

   Letting go of the negative ones would free you from the burden of having to carry them with you every day. It would also give you more opportunities to appreciate your life in general.

Case Study

Though Amy had begun keeping a list of her blessings, she felt like she was not taking a proactive approach to her happiness. At this point, she was only waiting until something good had happened to her.

To live her best life, Amy started forming a happiness plan. Using her knowledge about effective task management and goal setting, she identified the various ways she can seek out happiness in everything she did.

Feeling more satisfied with this approach, Amy set out to implement her plan to be happier not just at work but in all important areas of her life.

Practice Test

Create your happiness plan using the following table format. You may choose only one area in your life to focus on this exercise. However, feel free to explore all the ways you can think of, as long as you would follow through with the prescribed format.

Area	Goal	Action Plan (To-Do List)
		1.
		2.

3.

1.

2.

3.

1.

2.

3.

Once you have created your plan, answer the following questions:

- Why did you choose these particular areas (s) in your life to be included in the happiness plan?

- Evaluate your happiness goal vis-à-vis the S.M.A.R.T. goal criteria:

    o Specific?
    _____
    _____
    _____

- Measureable?

  _____
  _____
  _____

- Achievable?

  _____
  _____
  _____

- Realistic?

  _____
  _____
  _____

- Time-Bound?

  _____
  _____
  _____

• Based on how well you have made your goals, how do you feel about the happiness action plan that you have made?

Chapter 10

Reach Out to Someone

People suffering from anxiety find it hard to seek out for help due to various reasons. Their tendency to overthink keeps them from acting upon their need for help. They also become more bound to the stigmas associated with mental health issues.

Moreover, the negative thoughts may prevent them from voicing out their concerns out of fear and paranoia, both of which are typically rooted in stigmas and the kind of mental conditioning they have had in their life. This would then translate to worries about being rejected by the people around them and being isolated from those they care about.

In case you are one of these people, know that there are plenty of ways to ask for help. The most accessible one is through the support of your family and friends. However, if you are not comfortable with that, then affordable—sometimes free—therapies conducted with the guidance of a mental health expert are also available nowadays. There are even methods now that allow people to speak out anonymously.

To help you better identify the many ways you can reach out to someone about your mental health issues, the following sections cover the important things you need to keep in mind, especially during challenging times.

Don't be Afraid to Ask for Help

Getting over your fear and worries about reaching out to others is a crucial step in stopping yourself from engaging in overthinking and feeling anxious. As mentioned earlier, the most accessible group of people that you can connect with are those who love you and care about your wellbeing.

To guide you through this, here are the steps you need to take to start effectively communicating with them about this sensitive topic.

- Identify the members of your family and friends that you can trust.
- Schedule a private chat with them on a date and time that is convenient for both of you.
- Open up an honest conversation by admitting that you need help in overcoming your tendency

to overthink, your feelings of anxiety, your negative thoughts, and your worries.

- Describe in detail how these mental issues are affecting you in terms of the important aspects of your life, such as your relationships, vocation, and health.

- Be specific about what you need from them so that they can offer you better support.

- Share your safety plan with them so that they will know what to do in case you suffer from panic attacks or any other severe side-effects.

- Promise to keep them up to date about your goal to overcome these issues.

If you are not ready to lay all of these out to the people who know you personally, then you may try joining support groups that are composed of other people who are suffering from similar issues.

In these groups, confidentiality is of the utmost importance to make every member feel safe whenever they open up about their personal experiences. It takes a different kind of courage to admit to strangers the troubles and mistakes in your life. However, the following benefits of doing so typically outweigh these reservations.

- You will likely feel less judged and more understood.

- You are actively encouraged to be open and honest about your thoughts and feelings, no matter how dark and depressing they are.

- The other members are going to share practical tips that have worked for them, and thus may work for you.

- You will get access to relevant resources, such as self-help books and therapists, that can help you resolve your issues.

- After some time, you might feel less lonely and isolated.

Take note that it may take you a while before you can find a support group that will match your needs and preferences. Fortunately, there are plenty of ways to find one that might be compatible with you. You may search online for existing support groups near you, or you may try checking local mental health centers for recommendations. If you are comfortable asking your trusted family members and friends about this, then you may also ask for their advice.

Talk to a Physician If Everything Else Fails

If talking to your loved ones and support groups do not cause any significant improvements, then seriously consider seeking the help of mental health professional.

There are various types of physicians and therapists that you can look for. Each one has its own specialty, but most people who suffer from overthinking and anxiety are advised to get help from those with a background in cognitive-behavioral therapy. This branch of psychology is considered by many as one of the more effective approaches to mental health issues.

Much like support groups, it can be challenging to find a therapist that is compatible with you. You can start finding one through the same methods you have employed in searching for support groups.

Some therapists offer phone consultations so that you can try their services out first before committing to a series of therapy sessions. In case you are not comfortable speaking on the phone with a relative stranger, then an email consultation with a therapist is also pretty common nowadays.

Case Study

Amy has still not resolved her issues with her colleagues at this point. Since her first plan did not work as intended, she sought the help of her best friend, Danny.

After confiding in him about her experiences at work, Amy was surprised to find out that Danny had faced similar challenges when he was just starting at the architectural firm he is working at.

Although different settings, Danny shared with Amy some tips on how he had handled the situation back then. He had also reminded her that she did not have to please everybody and that their opinions would only matter if she would let them get to her.

Feeling well supported and understood, Amy felt more confident that she could get through this issue as well as Danny had done. If not, she knew that he would always have her back.

Practice Test

Answer the following questions about this interaction between Amy and Danny:

- Was Amy right about confiding her work problems to her best friend, Danny? Why or why not?

- Are Danny's pieces of advice actionable for Amy? How do you think Amy would translate Danny's advice into her goals and to-do list?

- Based on all that you have learned so far from this book, what advice would you give to Amy, aside from the ones given already by Danny?

Conclusion

"No one saves us but ourselves. No one can, and no one may. We ourselves must walk the path."

– Buddha

I'd like to thank you and congratulate you for transiting my lines from start to finish.

I hope this book was able to help you understand the causes and effects of overthinking, anxiety, negative thoughts, and worrying in different aspects of your life. I also hope that you were able to find a useful technique that can help you overcome them once and for all.

At this point, you are now better equipped to take control of your thoughts and emotions. In this book, you have learned how to:

- Accept the past, live in the present, and plan better for the future;
- Follow through on your tasks and plans up to completion;

- Optimize your home, relationships, work-life, digital space, and health;

- Set significant and achievable goals in your life; and

- Be more open and honest about your thoughts and feeling to the people who are willing to help you through this.

The next step is to maintain your personal journal as you apply your preferred techniques that have been discussed in the previous chapters of this book. You are free to experiment with which of these strategies would work best with your needs and current situation.

Finally, I want you to take responsibility for your personal wellbeing. Take charge of finding a way to stop overthinking and overcome your anxieties, negative thoughts, and worries by following through with any applicable techniques discussed in the previous chapters. Since you know yourself best—your strengths, limitations, and fears—you know better than anyone which techniques would get you closer to a future that is free from paralyzing thoughts and negative vibes.

Remember, "Knowing is not enough; we must apply. Willing is not enough; we must do", a quote by Goethe.

I wish you the very best!

A Short message from the Author

Hey, I hope you are enjoying the book? I would love to hear your thoughts!

Many readers do not know how hard reviews are to come by and how much they help an author.

I would be incredibly grateful if you could take just 60 seconds to write a short review on the product page of this book, even if it is a few sentences!

Thanks for the time taken to share your thoughts!

Your review will genuinely make a difference for me and help gain exposure for my work.

Your review will genuinely make a difference for me and help gain exposure for my work.

PART II

The Secrets of Vagus Nerve Stimulation

18 Proven, Science-Backed Exercises and Methods to Activate Your Vagal Tone and Overcome Inflammation, Chronic Stress, Anxiety, Epilepsy, and Depression.

Introduction

It is no surprise that most people have not heard of the vagus nerve. With such a name, there is little wonder. Even though the vagus nerve is often overlooked, this nerve plays a significant role in your body and nervous system than you can ever imagine. The vagus nerve is the longest of all the nerves in your body, and it is linked to several parts of your body. It starts in the brain and travels around the body, regulating the control of your digestive system, liver, spleen, pancreas, gallbladder, kidneys, stomach, throat muscles, small intestine, heart, lungs and some part of your large intestine. It works closely with your autonomic nervous system, most especially, your parasympathetic nervous system (what is called your rest and digest state). For instance, the vagus nerve knows when your heart rate increases from an energy-consuming or stressful activity, and immediately, it activates your parasympathetic system which then prepares your body for rest and ensures among others that;

- Your blood pressure is reduced, and all associated conditions such as stroke and heart disease are less likely to occur.

- Your digestive system is more efficient in a way that you don't bloat or become unable to process food.

- Your body produces more enzymes to break down food.

- Your body can regulate blood sugar levels more efficiently that you are at a lower risk of having type 2 diabetes.

- Your body can respond to inflammation, thereby reducing the possibility of related diseases such as IBS, arthritis, lupus, and more.

- Your chance of headaches and migraine are reduced.

- Your mood improves, and
- You feel more relaxed to deal with depression and anxiety.

How well your vagus nerve performs is determinant on the health of your body. The opposite happens when the vagus nerve is not able to support your body and keep you healthy in stressful situations. This would lead to an overactivation of your parasympathetic nervous system, which in turn activates the sympathetic nervous system (fight or flight state) to take over your body. Under consistent and uncontrolled stress levels, our body becomes susceptible to a range of problems such as;

- High blood pressure
- Type -2 diabetes
- Strokes
- Heart disease

- Poor digestion
- Obesity
- Respiratory failure
- Inflammatory disease, such as IBS, arthritis, lupus, etc.
- Depression, and more.

How possible it is you may ask, that these issues which are on the increase in today's modern world, are associated with the malfunctioning of the vagus nerve?

The answer is quite simple. Given that the vagus nerve originates from the brainstem, which is inside your brain and branches out to connect several organs and parts of your body that is responsible for keeping you healthy, any damage to this nerve inadvertently affects the functioning of your organs and your overall health. This damage can be as a result of certain harmful medications used to treat a disease or illness. It could be an injury, an accident, or a surgery that affected this nerve. It could also be the type of food you eat, your kind of lifestyle such as having too much alcohol or excessive smoking, or even something simple as not regularly exercising that could cause damage to this nerve – whichever the case, the result can alter your health and life for the worse. I know this because it happened to me, and I never knew the malfunctioning of this nerve was the cause of my predicament until my quest for a solution led me to a deeper understanding of the vagus nerve and its impact on my health.

Now more than ever, recognizing the role played by your vagus nerve on your overall health and wellbeing is increasingly important and requires that active measures be taken to tend to this nerve.

You don't have to go through what I experienced to understand the importance of this nerve, and why it needs to be cared for. Perhaps you already found yourself in a messy state of health, and you are experiencing one or more of the defects associated with a damaged vagus nerve, you don't have to worry because this book would:

- Enlighten you on several health conditions that is linked to a damaged vagus nerve.

- Describe science-backed exercises and practices, and passive methods of stimulation you can start right away to strengthen your vagus nerve.

- Help you to stimulate and unlock the power of your vagus nerve to heal your body.

- Show you some vital foods and supplements you should take for a healthy vagus nerve.

- Reveal certain substances and lifestyle habits that can damage your vagus nerve and,

- Empower you to take full control of your health and overall wellbeing.

Thank you for downloading this book, I hope you enjoy it!

Chapter 1

Getting to Know Your Vagus Nerve

Picture yourself at home on a Saturday evening after a hectic day. Perhaps to recover from the stress encountered during the day, you decided to give yourself a treat by eating a deliciously cooked meal, and now sitting on your couch to unwind and relax. At this point, you feel wholesomely at rest, so much that you are unaware of how you dozed off so suddenly and falling into a deep sleep. Now while asleep and in your subconscious, you may be thinking your body is as relaxed as you are, whereas a division of your nervous system is actively at work. This division of your nervous system at work, while you are far asleep, is the parasympathetic nervous system, which is busy reducing your heart rate, regulating your breathing, and marching orders to your digestive system organs.

One particular nerve that is heavily involved with the parasympathetic nervous system is the Vagus Nerve (VN).

Our nervous system is made up of about 100 billion nerve cells, which releases information from the brain to the body and vice versa. The vagus nerve is one of the most critical command center responsible for bi-directional communication between the brain and the body. A nerve probably 90% of the population have never heard of or have no clue of its location, nor how powerful this nerve is to the human body. How is it possible that a single nerve that emanates from the brainstem is the longest of all the 12 cranial nerves that connect to the essential organs of the body? Have you ever wondered what could happen to your body should this delicate nerve suffer an injury or gets damaged?

So then, join me and find out.

What is the Vagus Nerve?

Vagus in Latin means "to wander," simply because the vagus nerve wanders from the brain into the body i.e., from the brainstem linking the neck, thorax (chest), and abdomen (belly). The vagus nerve, also referred to as the 10th cranial nerve or cranial nerve X, is not only the longest nerve, but also the most complicated nerve of the 12 pairs of cranial nerves that branches out from the brain.

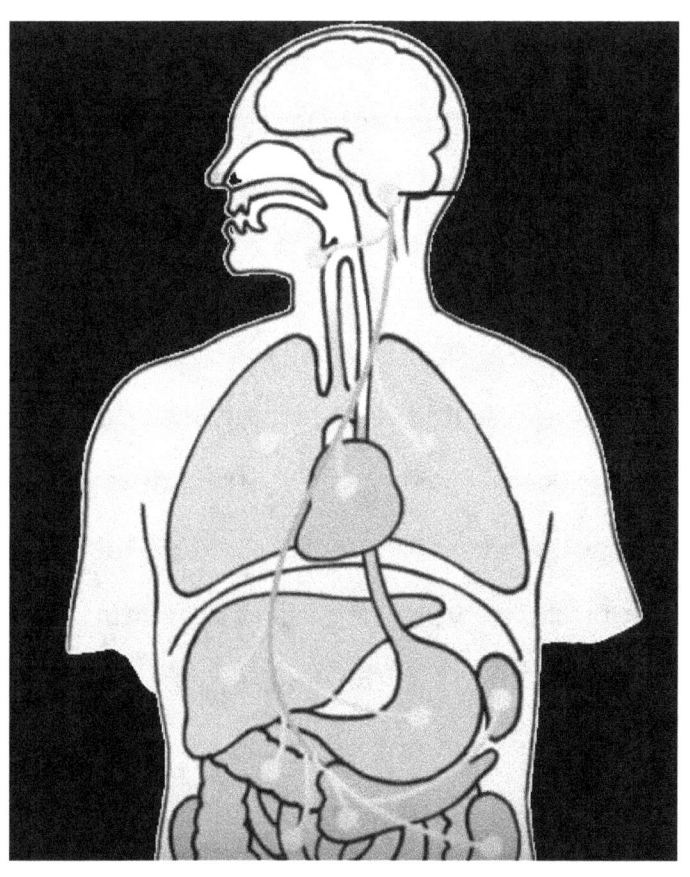

Our body is made up primarily of two nervous systems: the central nervous system and the peripheral nervous system. The latter is further subdivided into the somatic nervous system and the autonomic nervous system. The autonomic nervous system comprises; the sympathetic and the parasympathetic nervous system. The former functions as a "fight or flight" system, just like the gas pedal in an automobile that gears you up to keep firing.

The parasympathetic nervous system, on the other hand, works in the opposite direction. It functions as a "rest and digest" system by slowing you down just like your car brakes – using neurotransmitters such as acetylcholine to reduce your heart rate, blood pressure, and to slow down your organs. The command center for the functioning of the parasympathetic nervous system is your vagus nerve. It is safe to conclude that your vagus nerve is the commander-in-chief when it comes to receiving grace under pressure. It is not the only nerve found in the parasympathetic nervous system, but it is, to a large extent, the most critical nerve since it has the most far-reaching effects on the human body.

Activating the rest and digest state of the parasympathetic nervous system is just one of the many functions performed by the vagus nerve. It is also responsible for facilitating the involuntary (autonomic) activities of the body which includes among others:

- Breathing
- Speech
- Swallowing
- Heartbeat
- Blood Pressure
- Hearing
- Taste
- Blood Circulation
- Digestion
- Bladder Movement
- Sexual Arousal and;

- Gut Health

Although your vagus nerve is the commander-in-chief of receiving grace under pressure, damage to the vagus nerve can cause the parasympathetic response to a fight or flight situation to backfire. For instance, anytime you pull your yourself off a crucial event, feel insecure or intimidated, your vagus nerve would interpret it to mean you are in real danger, thereby exacerbating the situation.

Have you ever asked yourself why you experience the physical symptoms of performance anxiety like a racing heart, sweaty palms, stomach upset, dry mouth, and shaky feeling? These are signs that your vagus nerve is malfunctioning and disengaging. In the absence of a healthy vagus nerve, we only end up having access to parts of our brain that controls primary instincts like fear and fight or flight response.

The healthy functioning of the vagus nerve can be impaired by stress, anxiety, smoking, alcoholism, poor diet, lack of exercise and sleep, or even having part of the nerve accidentally damage during surgery.

When the vagus nerve is not able to perform to the best of its ability, the body and mind become susceptible to a range of conditions which includes but are not limited to:

- Depression
- Anxiety Disorders
- Obesity
- Cardiovascular Disorders
- Hypertension
- Diabetes
- Digestive Disorders

- Chronic Inflammation
- Kidney Malfunction and;
- Parkinson's Disease

Luckily, you can harness the power of your vagus nerve and keep it engaged to release grace when under pressure. When you understand the incredible power your vagus nerve has, you would be geared not only to start practicing ways to exercise its strength to keep you at rest when in distress but also to keep you healthy – physically and mentally.

Anatomy of the Vagus Nerve

As much as possible without being very technical, I would explain the origin of the vagus nerve, and its structural form as it travels all the way through to the organs where it innervates and sends information to and from the brain.

From the Brainstem Connections

The neurons that give rise to the vagus nerve starts in the brainstem, which stems from four nuclei – the dorsal motor nucleus, ambiguous nucleus, solitary nucleus, and spinal trigeminal nucleus. Each of one these exercise control over certain fibers of the nerve. The sensory neurons retrieve signals directly from the skin, which the vagus nerve innervates to the spinal trigeminal nucleus (it includes a certain part of the ear skin, which plays an important role when the vagus nerve is activated using acupuncture treatment). The vagus nerve brings the signals from the internal organs to the solitary nucleus, which are then taken to the brain for further processing. Examples of these signals are those from the stomach, lungs, heart, intestinal tract, gall bladder, liver, spleen, and pancreas. Our body can also pass direct signals to these organs via the vagus nerve by the parasympathetic fibers – originating from the dorsal motor nucleus. These signals are necessary because they provide support in calming and regulating the function of the heart and lungs, while also increasing the actions of the gut and intestinal tract, pancreas, liver, spleen, and gallbladder.

Neurons that perform a motor function, especially to control most of the muscles (the muscles which ensure the airway is kept open, as well as producing sound using the vocal cords) found in the throat and upper airway, are sent out by the nuclei called nucleus ambiguous.

It is important to note that the only nerves in the human body with four separate functions and separate nuclei that contributes to the component fibers are the right and left vagus. On the other hand, the majority of the other nerves found in the human body carry simple sensory information from the skin to the muscles. This differentiation only goes to show how vital the vagus nerve truly is and how extensive its functions are in the human body.

Having looked at the vagus nerve from the brainstem, let's replicate same for the neck, thorax (chest area), and abdomen (belly or tummy area).

Down to the Neck

Right from the medulla oblongata (resident in the brainstem), fibers of the left and right vagus nerves extend directly to the cranial cavity (the inside of the skull), converging to form what is called the vagus nerve – this then passes out of the skull via an opening (the jugular foramen). This jugular foramen is a vast space between the neck and the skull that provides room for the vagus nerve and other blood vessels to pass through. Once the vagus nerve exits the skull, it then enters the upper neck just behind the ear, which sits in-between two blood vessels i.e., the internal carotid artery and the internal jugular vein – our blood's direct lines to and from the brain. The location of the vagus nerve just close to these two blood vessels goes to show how critical this 10th cranial nerve is. Damage of this nerve would most certainly lead to inadequate functioning of most organs of the body, while damage to the blood vessels can result in an outright death. Just after the vagus passes the jugular foramen, exists a thickening of the vagus nerve referred to as the superior ganglion (or jugular ganglion) – a nerve's thickening, formed by a group of sensory neuron cell bodies very close to each other. These cell bodies congregate inside the ganglion, reforming into the thinner nerve section, thereby paving the way for the first branch of the vagus nerve called the auricular branch.

The auricular branch goes back into the skull via the mastoid canaliculus (an opening) toward the ear via another opening of the skull, the tympanomastoid fissure. The auricular branch is sensitive to touch, wetness, and temperature felt on the skin of the ear most especially, the external canal, auricle, and tragus – the major target for activating the treatment of the VN dysfunction with the aid of auricular acupuncture (acupuncture is directed to the ear, and is discussed in more details later in this book).

Just as the vagus nerve starts to pass downward from the superior ganglion, the VN thickens once more, giving rise to the inferior ganglion (also referred to as the nodose ganglion) – which houses the cell bodies of the neurons involved in retrieving information from the internal organs. The vagus nerve again thins out and instantly goes into a passageway made by the carotid sheath (a thickening of connective tissue). In the carotid sheath, the vagus nerve goes into its next branch called the pharyngeal branch. Although this branch has neurons that come directly from the vagus nerve, it also provides some supporting neurons from the ninth and eleventh cranial nerves. As soon as these neurons meet, they will go through the midline of the body until they get to the upper part of the throat (the pharynx). In the pharynx, motor signals are sent to several muscles by the vagus nerve. These muscles play a role in swallowing, in the opening and closing of the upper airway, as well as in the maintenance of the gag reflex. The vagus nerve goes into its third branch (the superior laryngeal nerve) as it travels down the sides of the neck. Immediately, the superior laryngeal nerve branches from the VN after the pharyngeal branch, providing motor signals to the muscles of the larynx. These muscles are responsible for controlling your voice's pitch. As the VN further goes down via the carotid sheath, the cervical cardiac branches arise – the two of three branches innervating the heart, while the third branch (thoracic cardiac branch) appears just after exiting the carotid sheath in the thorax (chest).

These branches interrelate with the nerves of the sympathetic nervous system and form the cardiac plexus (plexi as its plural form). Plexi is made up of a collection of intermingling nerve fibers of several branches and several origin nerves that traverses toward a targeted area). There are two cardiac plexi – the superficial cardiac plexus, located in front of the aorta, and the deep cardiac plexus, located at the back of the aorta (aorta is the main blood vessel that transports blood from the heart to other parts of the human body). At this point, one vital thing to take note of is that the fibers of the cardiac plexi control the rate of the electrical activity responsible for pumping your heart.

Down to the Thorax

Upon exiting the carotid sheath, the vagus nerve goes right down into the thorax, specifically at the back of the first and second ribs, as well as in the front of the wider blood vessels extending from the heart. The left vagus nerve goes in front of the aorta (at the arch), which then gives rise to its fourth branch (the left side recurrent laryngeal nerve). Right across the other side of the body, the right vagus nerve takes a similar route, but instead, it goes in front of the right subclavian artery, sending off its fourth branch (the right side recurrent laryngeal nerve). These branches convey motor signals directly from the brainstem to the muscles of the larynx, which are vital to produce your vocal sounds. Once the vagus nerves get to where the aorta is, the left and right of its nerves sendoff branches to the pair of lungs. A pulmonary branch channeled to the anterior pulmonary plexus is sent by the left vagus nerve, while a pulmonary branch channeled to the posterior pulmonary plexus is sent by the right vagus nerve. The nerve branches mingle with sympathetic neurons, regroups, and after that, travels to innervate the lungs on each side. Based on what the body needs, these branches would navigate its way to the bronchi and the broader branches of the lungs, opening and closing them accordingly.

Down to the Abdomen

The organs of the abdomen are the last section that the vagus nerve innervates. These organs are very critical to the human body because it aids digestion, controls the immune system, and prevents the blood supplied to our cells from having any form of toxins that could affect the health of our cells.

The stomach is the first branch of the abdomen where the vagus nerve goes. The muscles of the stomach are stimulated to function by the vagus nerve fibers when the body is in the rest and digest state. Signals are sent to the parietal cells by the vagus nerve to secrete hydrochloric acid, to the chief cells to secrete digestive enzymes (pepsin and gastrin), and to the stomach's muscle cells to churn and push the food in the stomach into the small intestine. If there is damage to the vagus nerve and these vital signals to the stomach's cells are not being sent, problems such as hypochlorhydria, or what is called low stomach acid will arise – a major root cause of several health issues.

The liver is the second branch of the abdomen, where the vagus nerve goes. These branches are responsible for the sensations you feel when hungry. The food we eat first goes to the stomach where it is broken down, and from there, it goes to the small intestine, where the majority of our macronutrients such as fats, amino acids, and carbohydrates are absorbed into the bloodstream. These nutrients then travel into the liver where they are filtered, processed, and prepared for transporting signals back to the brain. From the liver, information is relayed to the brain by the vagus nerve concerning blood sugar balance, fat intake, as well as the general functioning of the liver. Information concerning the amount of bile required to aid in the digestion of fats can also be relayed to the brain. The liver performs several functions that require the input of the vagus nerve, which includes but not limited to the production of bile and bile salts; production of glucose for balancing the blood sugar; and managing hunger and satiety. Generally speaking, the liver is very vital to our overall wellbeing. However, the innervation of the vagus nerve plays a major role in keeping this balance. The gallbladder, which is closely linked with the liver is very vital for the maximum functioning of our bodies. When our liver creates what is known as bile and bile salts, they are then transported to the gallbladder, where they are stored in preparation for our next meal. As soon as we start our next meal, bile is then pumped by the gallbladder into the first part of the small intestine (the duodenum), which helps to transport fats into the bloodstream. The vagus nerve, yet again, is responsible for mediating the pumping by the gallbladder. From the liver, the vagus never courses to send signals to the gallbladder, and in the process, it activates the muscle cells in its walls, which then pumps bile into the digestive tract.

The pancreas being the next branch of the vagus nerve, is one of the most vital glands in our body, having both an endocrine and exocrine component. The endocrine part of the pancreas secretes insulin and glucagon into the bloodstream, which helps to balance the level of glucose in the blood. The exocrine component of the pancreas, on the other hand, secretes digestive enzymes via a duct into the small intestine. These digestive enzymes are protease (which breaks down proteins into amino acids), lipase (which breaks down fats into fatty acids and cholesterol), and amylase (which breaks down carbohydrates into sugars). The innervation of the vagus nerve transports signals from the pancreas to the brainstem, in which information about the cell status of the endocrine and exocrine are relayed. Information that pertains to the intake of food, as well as the enzymes required to be produced and released into the bloodstream and digestive tract, are also relayed from the brainstem to the organ – the innervation of the vagus nerve is vital for transmitting this information. As soon as the vagus nerve travels past the stomach, the celiac plexus is then formed (a network that exists between the lumbar sympathetic nerves and the parasympathetic fibers of the vagus nerve). This network sends branches to the other parts of the organs in the abdomen. The spleen is the first organ that is innervated after the celiac plexus. The location of the spleen can be traced to the left side of your body, below your left lung, which is opposite your liver. The spleen is responsible for monitoring the bloodstream, as well as the activation or deactivation of the cells of the immune system based on the senses it receives. The sympathetic branch of the nervous system sends information to the spleen to activate the inflammatory pathways, turning on responses to any physical and biochemical trauma or damage. On the other hand, the parasympathetic branch of the nervous system sends information to the spleen to halt the inflammation processes – an area where the vagus nerve is also actively involved.

After the celiac plexus, the next branch of the vagus nerve courses to the small intestine. As soon as the food is churned in the stomach by chemical and physical processes, it then travels to the small intestine where the pancreatic digestive enzymes and bile further process it. The small intestine functions by breaking down and absorbing most of our body's macronutrients, which include fats, proteins, and carbohydrates. The macronutrients which the lining cells of the small intestine have accepted are also received by the bloodstream. When we take in bites of food (called chyme in the digestive process), it is pushed down the length of the small intestine. For this to occur, the muscle cells of the digestive tract are first activated by the vagus nerve by sending signals to the network of nerves lining the gut – these networks of nerves lining the gut are referred to as the enteric nervous system. The bacteria in our body have a significant relationship with the rest of the cells that live in our digestive tracts, i.e., the symbiotic relationship of our human cells with the bacteria in our gut (the microbiome). Although most of our bacteria allies (which produces vital minerals, vitamins, and biochemical for us) are housed in the large intestine of the digestive tract, they can also generate several toxins and gas. The vagus nerve provides a relay path where the microbiome can communicate with our brain, which is very necessary to keep these bacteria in check, by signaling our brain on the functional status of the digestive tract and the microbiome. Approximately in the first half of the large intestine (the ascension and traverse colon) is where the vagus nerve innervates.

The last organ the vagus nerve innervates is the kidney. The function of the kidney (each located on the sides of the body) is to filter out fluid called urine – the blood pressure is a significant determinant of this control. The vagus nerve, which plays a significant role in controlling the function of the kidney, also plays a very vital role in managing the blood pressure. The vagus nerve does not just end at its course; instead, it gives rise to the last plexus with the parasympathetic nerve fibers that courses from the spinal cord's lower end. These fibers are what innervates the other half of the large intestine, which are the descending and sigmoid colon, the bladder, and the sex organs.

Why The Vagus Nerve Is So Important

The vagus nerve is one of the most vital nerves of the human body because it connects not only multiple organs, but also facilitates several processes that take place in our body by actively providing support to the workings of the autonomic nervous system. If you carefully followed me as I took on the anatomy of the vagus nerve in the previous section, you should have picked up several functions performed by this nerve.

Generally, the function of the vagus nerve is broken into four main parts:

Sensory

The sensory function of the vagus nerve is divided into two components, with each performing two different roles:

Somatic Component—This provides somatic sensations for the skin (i.e., sensations behind the ear or the outside area of the ear canal), as well as some regions of the throat.

Visceral Component—This provides visceral sensations experienced in the organs of the body (i.e., sensations for the heart, lungs, larynx, heart, esophagus, trachea, as well as a majority of the digestive tract).

Special Sensory

The vagus nerve plays a minor role in the taste sensation (i.e., taste sensation provided to the root of the tongue).

Motor

The motor function of the vagus nerve stimulates the muscles (responsible for swallowing and speech) in the pharynx, larynx, and the soft palate.

Parasympathetic

The parasympathetic function of the vagus nerve;

- Stimulates the muscles in the heart by regulating the heart rhythm

- Stimulates the muscles in the digestive tract to contract— which includes the stomach, esophagus, and most of the intestines, thereby paving the way for food to navigate through the tract.

Although the vagus nerve function is made up of four main parts, which I summarily touched on, I would go a little deeper into some of these functions.

Swallowing of Food

Whether you agree or not, swallowing is one of the most complex activity your body performs. This is true since it involves some intricate coordination between your brain and some specific nerves and muscles. For food swallowing to occur, the coordination of these muscles, pharynx (throat), larynx (voice box), and esophagus (the hollow tube that transports food from your throat to your stomach) is required. These muscles are all controlled by the cranial nerves, prominent amongst them is the vagus nerve – which allows for the swallowing of each bite of food by pausing the breathing reflex to prevent you from choking. The pharyngeal branch, as earlier discussed, is the second branch of the vagus nerve that manages the muscles of the pharynx. These muscles are the three constrictor muscles located behind the throat and the other two muscles that connects the throat to the soft palate (soft tissue behind the roof of the mouth). These muscles play a vital role in the pharyngeal phase of swallowing by pushing your chewed food down to the larynx as well as to the esophagus while keeping it away from the trachea, thereby ensuring your airway is cleared from food particles.

Promotes Digestion

The vagus nerve plays a significant role in managing the complex processes of your digestive system, which includes sending signals to the muscles of your stomach to contract and to push down the food into the small intestine. Your digestive system, in simple terms, relies on the vagus nerve to function correctly.

Let me give you a quick rundown of how the vagus nerve aids digestion beginning from your stomach all through to your intestines.

Stomach
Once the food swallowing process is completed and the food is pushed down your stomach, your vagus nerve would trigger the production of a certain amount of acid (gastric or stomach acid) in your stomach that helps to properly digest your food, kill bacteria, and absorb specific nutrient such as protein.

Pyloric Sphincter
The pyloric sphincter sits at the base of your stomach, allowing food (chyme) to exit the stomach into the intestines. The vagus nerve is responsible for triggering the opening and closing of the pyloric sphincter – this is

to ensure that the food does not stay in the stomach any longer than is necessary.

Gallbladder

The gallbladder, which connects to the bile duct of the liver, receives and stores bile, which, when released, helps with the proper digestion of fats contained in the food (chyme). The vagus nerve is responsible for stimulating the release of bile to the gall bladder and having both direct and indirect control over the functioning of the gall bladder.

Pancreas

The pancreas secretes digestive enzymes that help to digest and absorb nutrients in food, most importantly, fats, and proteins. Partial regulation of the pancreatic functions is achieved when the parasympathetic fiber innervates the pancreas (originating in the dorsal motor nucleus of the brain). This regulation is made possible by the vagus nerve, which also exercises direct control over the secretion of digestive enzymes.

Sphincter of Oddi

Sphincter of Oddi is a muscular valve that exercises control over the flow of bile and pancreatic enzymes into the small intestine. The vagus nerve stimulates the opening of the sphincter of Oddi to allow the flow of bile and pancreatic enzymes from the gallbladder and pancreas into the small intestine.

Intestines

Once the food (chyme) gets to the small and large intestine respectively, the vagus nerve would then stimulate the mixing and shifting of chyme, back and forth, allowing the proper absorption of nutrients into the bloodstream – this process is called peristalsis.

Without the proper functioning of the vagus nerve, proper peristalsis would not occur, which can lead to gastroparesis, bloating, constipation, and discomfort. If partially digested food remains in your intestines without being moved around, your body will absorb the toxins and free radicals that are produced, resulting in a potential chronic inflammation of the intestinal tract.

Fights Inflammation

The vagus nerve plays a vital role in fighting inflammation. A given amount of inflammation after an injury or infection is not out of place – this is the way our body notifies the immune system to heal and repair damaged tissue to protect our body against viruses and bacteria. However, if left uncontrolled and it gets out of hand, it could become chronic, leading to several autoimmune diseases such as rheumatoid arthritis and lupus. The vagus nerve is like a vast network of nerve fibers, positioned all around your organs like spies. When it receives the pro-inflammatory cytokine signal (substances the inflammatory cells secrete, affecting other cells) or a substance called tumor necrosis factor (TNF), it sends an alert to the brain to produce anti-inflammatory neurotransmitters which then regulate the body's immune response accordingly, thereby helping to manage stress and improving how the body responds to pain and illness.

Controls Heart Rate and Blood Pressure

The vagus nerve controls the heart rate and blood pressure through electrical impulses to the heart's natural pacemaker, the sinoatrial node (a group of cells in the wall of the heart's right atrium), where a neurotransmitter called acetylcholine is released to slow the pulse rate and blood pressure if it's too high, keeping a constant rhythm of the heart and thereby preventing tachycardia - a condition that causes your heart to beat more than 100 times per minute. By measuring the time interval between consecutive heartbeats over a given period of time, your heart rate variability (HRV) can be determined. The HRV data can provide valuable insights about the strength of your vagus nerve and the resilience of your heart.

Many studies have been reported on the benefits of stimulating the vagus nerve in patients with heart failure. A study conducted in 2011, as published in the European Heart Journal, reported that continuous stimulation of the vagus nerve could improve the efficiency of the heart to pump blood in patients suffering from heart failure. Similar results were reported in 2014 as published in the journal of cardiac failure where after six months of stimulating the vagus nerve of patients with heart failure, their heart pumped 4.5% more blood per beat than it did prior to the stimulation. More on the methods of vagus stimulation are covered in later sections of this book.

Facilitates Breathing

The vagus nerve pays close attention to how you breathe and sends a signal to the brain and heart to respond accordingly. When you breathe slowly, the oxygen demand of the heart muscle (myocardium) drops, and your heart rate reduces. In stressful situations, taking a slow deep breath would stimulate the vagus nerve to calm you down. If the vagus nerve does not stimulate the release of acetylcholine to the brain, your brain would be unable to communicate with your diaphragm (muscles at the base of your chest which contracts and forces your lungs to expand and take in air), and you won't be able to breath – this would essentially lead to death so to speak. This is why exposing your body to Botox, and mercury most especially can potentially cause severe damage to your vagus nerve, because it interrupts the production of acetylcholine.

Provides Ear Sensations

As earlier discussed in the anatomy of the vagus nerve, the auricular branch (the first branch of the vagus nerve), helps in providing sensations such as touch, wetness, and temperature to certain areas of the ear (e.g., the external canal, auricle, and tragus areas). This is very important because sensations of the ear can be stimulated by the vagus nerve when the auricular acupuncture method of stimulation is used.

Manages Hunger and Satiety

Has it ever crossed your mind why some people get full so easily after eating a small amount of food, and other people still feel hungry not until they have eaten a large amount of food? This is your vagus nerve at work.

The vagus nerve, as we know, connects your gut to your brain, and one type of signal that travels up and down the vagus nerve via this connection is the hunger and satiety signal.

This is how it works…

In the course of eating a meal, the quantity of food present in your stomach stimulates the vagus nerve to send satiety signals to your brain. Your brain then flips by saying, "full." This is how you stop feeling hungry after a meal.

Your gut contains several nutrient-sensing receptors that recognize when you have gotten enough of certain nutrients such as carbohydrates, proteins, and fats. These nutrient-sensing receptors include serotonin, ghrelin, and gustducin. These receptors may or may not be activated, which depends on whether the food you eat contains those nutrients. Vagus nerve is the means by which your brain receives the hunger or satiety nutrient signal. However, when the vagus nerve is damaged and underperforms, those vital satiety signals from your stomach and the intestines would not be able to travel back to your brain. The implication of this is that you would more than likely exhibit a continuous feeling of hunger, lack of satiety, and end up overeating in the process.

Let me paint a clearer picture of what I am trying to communicate...

Remember the nutrient receptors I mentioned earlier? One of such receptors that sense glucose is gustducin (a glucose taste receptor in your gut). A damaged vagus nerve can prevent this receptor from sending signals to the brain that you've had enough sugars and carbs, which could essentially lead to an overdose of glucose, impaired insulin secretion, and potentially resulting in obesity if the situation remains uncontrolled.

Gut-Brain Communication

Does going with your "gut feelings" to make a decision sounds familiar to you? Or have you ever felt "butterflies in your stomach" when you are nervous? If you have experienced any of these, then you are most likely receiving signals from the *second* brain (enteric nervous system) in your gut (specifically, your stomach and intestines).

Your "gut feelings" so to speak are signaled to the brain via the vagus nerve through electrical impulses. It is often said that the vagus nerve cells are 80% afferent, meaning your brain receives more signals from your body while only 20% are efferent, i.e., your brain sends fewer signals to your body – the reason why the term body-mind connection is often used.

In your gut lies what is called the microbiome (tens of trillions of bacteria composition and other micro-organisms). These microbiomes play a very important role by enabling the release of critical neurotransmitters such as Serotonin, GABA, and Dopamine that regulates your mood, thinking capabilities, and memory, among many others. So, for instance, whenever you experience any emotions or sensations in your body, be it a broken heart, anger, sadness, anxiety, or happiness, your gut microbiome is more than likely the reason for this. You experience these emotions because these neurotransmitters in your body have sent signals to your brain through your vagus nerve. This communication system between your gut and your brain is what is referred to as the gut-brain axis.

The feedback loop between the gut, vagus nerve, and the brain goes beyond our emotions or sensations.

Several other signals are sent along this axis. The goings-on in our guts can, as a matter of fact, be a life or death situation. If the gut is empty, the vagus nerve must inform the brain; if the gut has a problem that will hinder the processing of food and nutrition absorption, the brain must be notified; if the gut is being attacked by pathogens, the brain needs to be in the loop – with status report being constantly updated between the gut and brain.

Think of the vagus nerve as that superhighway communication that ensures your body is in constant touch with your brain. Given that the vagus nerve operates in tandem with the gut microbiome to facilitate the gut-brain communication, it has become increasingly important to not only take proper care of your vagus nerve but also your gut health by engaging in gut-friendly practices such as:

- Taking probiotic supplements or eating fermented foods rich in probiotics such as yogurt, kefir, sauerkraut, cheese, kimchi, sauerkraut, kombucha, and miso

- Avoiding the use of certain antibiotics

- Less consumption of sugary foods and artificial sweeteners

- Regular exercise

- Getting enough sleep

- Cutting down on diets with animal fat

- Eating foods with omega-3 fats and;

- Eating more prebiotic-fiber foods such as asparagus, bananas, chicory, garlic, Jerusalem artichoke, onions, and whole grains.

Note: Some of the above are covered in detail toward the tail end of this book.

Chapter 2

Vagal Tone and Why It Matters

The vagus nerve activity of some people is healthier and stronger than others, which allows their bodies to quickly relax after a stressful activity.

For example, the stress you go through when you subject your body to a high degree of exercise is good, especially when you are done with the exercise, and your body gains health and strength – giving you a positive mental feeling of your achievement. Another example is the positive feeling you get when you complete a stressful task, the feeling of "yes, I did it!". This feeling of accomplishment will gear you up as you prepare for subsequent stressful assignments knowing that you have the situation under control.

The point I am passing across is that a repetitive positive fight or flight response is good if a positive emotion is associated with the completion of the stressful event. Nonetheless, continuous fight or flight response becomes unhealthy if no positive result is associated with the event. Examples of such event are found in our everyday life which includes work, school, finance, and family – falling short in these areas could easily run us down. The impact of this would result in a low vagal tone, which, if sustained for an extended period of time, may lead to poor health and performance.

Please bear in mind that other factors can also cause a low vagal tone, such as poor lifestyle habits, while vagus-friendly habits can increase your vagal tone. In other words, the strength of your vagus response or the degree to which your vagus nerve is active is known as your vagal tone.

It is also interesting to know that based on studies carried out in this area, vagal tone is passed on from mother to child. The implication is that mothers who experience depression, anxiety, or feel angry during their pregnancy have lower vagal activity. And as soon as their child is birthed, the newborn would also have low vagal activity coupled with low dopamine and serotonin levels.

High Vagal Tone – What it Relates to

How strong your vagal tone is would determine how strong your body would function. A high vagal tone would improve your body systems, such as regulating your blood sugar levels, reducing the risk of diabetes, stroke, cardiovascular disease, and migraines, and improving your digestion, among others. A high vagal tone is also associated with better mood, more resilience to stress, and less anxiety. A vagal tone that is high is a pointer to a high heart rate variability (more on this is discussed in the subsequent section).

Low Vagal Tone – What it Relates to

Having a low vagal tone simply means the strength of your vagus nerve response is low. Having a low vagus response could lead to several health conditions such as cardiovascular diseases, strokes, diabetes, depression, negative moods, chronic fatigue, and a higher chance of being affected by inflammations such as autoimmune diseases (rheumatoid arthritis, inflammatory bowel disease, and more). A low vagal tone points to a low heart rate variability.

For instance, a study shows that people with inflammatory conditions most times have low heart rate variability, which can trigger the release of pro-inflammatory cytokines, leading to increased sympathetic nervous system activity and stress hormones.

Measuring Your Vagal Tone

Vagal tone is measured when you track your heart rate alongside your breathing rate. Your heart rate increases when you breathe in and decreases when you breathe out. The difference between the heart rate inhalation and heart rate exhalation is your vagal tone. This difference by the standard is called the heart rate variability. Consequently, to determine if your vagal tone is either low or high, you first have to measure the variation of time (in milliseconds) between consecutive heartbeats, called the heart rate variability (HRV) – a golden standard in measuring the strength of the vagal tone.

What is Heart Rate Variability?

Heart rate variability can be traced to our autonomic nervous system, divided into the sympathetic (fight or flight) and the parasympathetic (rest and digest) nervous system, and is responsible for regulating important body systems such as our heart rate, breathing, blood pressure, and digestion. Heart rate variability is a pointer that both nervous systems are functioning.

Intrinsic heart rate is the measurement of a condition where there is no regulation by neither the parasympathetic nor sympathetic nervous system. When the intrinsic heart rate is prevented from autonomic regulation, a healthy heart contracts within the range of 60-100 beats per minute.

Regulation by the parasympathetic nervous system reduces your heart rate from the intrinsic level while providing variability between successive heartbeats. Parasympathetic regulation almost instantly affects a change on a few heartbeats at a time, after which the heart rate reverts to the intrinsic rate. Sympathetic regulation, on the other hand, increases your heart rate from the intrinsic rate, with little or no room for variability between successive heartbeats. Several consecutive heartbeats are affected by the regulation of the sympathetic nervous system.

The implication of this is that when a person is in the rest and digest response state, the heart rate would be lower but with a higher HRV while in a fight or flight response state, the heart rate would be higher but with a lower HRV.

Factors such as stress can cause the parasympathetic nervous system to be deactivated while activating the sympathetic nervous system even when you are resting.

Research over the years shows that people with a high HRV would exhibit greater cardiovascular fitness and with higher resilience to stress, while people with low HRV would manifest conditions such as depression, anxiety, and cardiovascular disease.

In general, HRV can provide you with feedback on your lifestyle, which can be a great way to determine how your nervous system is not only responding to the environment but also to your feelings, thoughts, and emotions.

Checking Your Heart Rate Variability

Healthy irregularities accompany a healthy heartbeat. Let's say your heart rate is 60 beats per minute; this does not imply your heart beats once in every second. A variation exists among the intervals between your heartbeats. For example, the interval between your successive heartbeats may be 0.5 ms between two consecutive beats and 1.5 ms between another two consecutive beats. Although the interval is measured in fractions of seconds, you can actually have a feel of the difference.

To have a sense of your HRV, place two fingers on your carotid artery (at the side of your neck) or on your wrist to find your pulse, and once you do, take deep breaths in and out. You will notice that the interval between your beats becomes longer (heart rate reduces) when you exhale while it becomes shorter (heart rate increases) when you inhale. Be aware that HRV can be influenced when exercising, which would create a much more consistent time lapse between beats. However, if at rest and you experience a high time variation between your breathing in and out, then it means you have a high HRV – a good sign of being able to cope with stress and a sign of having a good vagal tone (high vagal tone).

On the other hand, if at rest and you experience a low time variation between your breathing in and out, it means that you have a low HRV, mostly a fight or flight response to stress, which implies a low vagal tone – leading to your inability to cope with stress. If this state of low vagal tone persists for long, you will stand the risk of poor performance and health.

Although measuring your HRV using your pulse gives you a feel of what your HRV may be, it, however, does not provide you with an accurate HRV reading since it's difficult to detect actual variations in heartbeats without special technology. How you calculate your HRV is dependent on the technology, you wish to use.

One such common technology used today is the electrocardiogram (ECG) device. This device functions by picking up the electrical pulse from your heart's contraction. With the data retrieved, your HRV can be determined. Measuring your HRV using the ECG technology usually required you to visit a laboratory where complex machines and electrodes are placed over your body. But with technological advancement, this can simply be done at the comfort of your home using heart rate monitors such as the Polar H7 heart rate strap.

Also, a wearable smartwatch with an inbuilt ECG device has been validated in research as being a reliable method to measure your HRV. One such is the Apple Watch, which has been approved by the FDA. This even makes it very easy for lovers of Apple Watch to easily determine their HRV even on the go.

Another technology that doesn't use ECG to measure your HRV but instead requires an optical sensor to measure heartbeat intervals is the Photoplethysmography (PPG). PPG uses a light source and a photodetector at the surface of the skin to measure changes in blood volume. The well-known Oura ring uses PPG technology to determine the HRV.

The beauty of using either of these devices is that they are non-invasive which can be worn on your wrist, finger, or strapped around your chest to take measurement of your HRV even while asleep – this is very recommended because the longer the measurement while at rest with no distractions, the more reliable the data would be.

Interpreting Your Heart Rate Variability Result

There is no standard procedure for optimal HRV values, which is quite relatable given there are different methods to track and calculate it.

However, according to a 2016 study published in Health and Quality of Life Outcomes, low HRV are values that are <780ms while High HRV, as published in Sports Medicine Research, are values that are >=780 ms. HRV tends to be on the high side when a person is healthy and fit and how high this can be depend on the individual in question.

Because a number of factors such as age, gender, body functions, a person's lifestyle, and even hormones can affect the HRV reading, it is advisable that you do not compare your HRV value with that of others (even of the same gender). What you should rather do is focus on your own HRV and its trends. In addition, when using trends to compare your daily HRV values, measurement should be done using the same technology, and under similar conditions – preferably when sleeping at night since your body would be at rest.

Summing up, if the intervals of your heartbeat are constantly low, then you have a low HRV, and you would have a high HRV if the intervals are constantly high.

Increasing Your Vagal Tone

When your vagal tone is increased, it activates your parasympathetic nervous system, which for instance, would help your body relax faster after stress, your mood becomes more regulated, and your anxiety is better managed.

To a certain degree, the strength of your vagal tone is genetic, just like the mother who, during pregnancy, transferred her low vagal tone to her unborn child. This, however, does not imply that a low vagal tone cannot be changed and increased. Vagal tone can be increased using a number of methods such as undergoing some recommended natural exercises and practices e.g., deep breathing as well as the use of electrical stimulation methods, among others. Toward the tail end of this book, I would go deeper on these exercises and methods which you can use to increase your vagal tone.

Chapter 3

Conditions Associated with The Vagus Nerve

You probably are trying to understand why the dysfunction of the vagus nerve results in numerous diseases and health problems in the human body. Well, if you have assiduously followed my discussions from the beginning, you should already have your answer. The vagus nerve, as we already know, is the most complex cranial nerve, but not only that, it is also the largest network distribution of motor and sensory fibers within the human body compared to any of the 12 cranial nerves. It is as a result of this that the vagus nerve impacts a wide range of bodily functions such as gut-brain axis communication, neurotransmitter management, hormonal balance, and inflammation prevention, among many others. Therefore, any dysfunctions in the vagus nerve can have enormous effects throughout the body resulting in some of the many known diseases and health problems. That being said, it is important you know that most of these conditions outlined herein do not exist in isolation – meaning that if any of these conditions are taking place in the human body, it can also lead to further illness. For instance, obesity and inflammation are linked with cancers and diabetes just as anxiety or mood disorders could also result in depression.

Moving forward, let's take a look at some of the medical conditions that are associated with the vagus nerve.

Chronic Stress and Anxiety

When we subject ourselves to stressful situations such as the daily hassles of sitting in traffic for long hours, a pile of financial debt that keeps growing, stress arising from troubled relationships, unhappiness about your job, or even the stress to our body from the unhealthy foods we eat, the sympathetic nervous system becomes activated. If we are unable to turn off what activates the stress, not much time will pass by before these stress as little as it may seem compounds to become chronic stress, leading to health problems within our body. When we are stressed, two pathways become activated by the brain; the hypothalamus-pituitary-adrenal axis, and the brain-intestine axis.

During the fight or flight response, our brain would respond to stress and anxiety by increasing the production of Corticotropin-releasing hormone (CRF), the hormone involved in stress response. This hormone then travels from the hypothalamus to the pituitary gland, where they stimulate the release of adrenocorticotropic hormone (ACTH). This, in turn, then travels down the bloodstream to the adrenal glands to trigger cortisol and adrenaline induction – suppressors to our body's immune system and precursors of inflammation. This explains the reason why we easily fall ill when we are stressed and anxious, and eventually fall into depression, a mental disorder linked to inflammatory brain response. When cortisol is produced in a large amount, it causes the volume of the hippocampus to be reduced – this is the part of our brain that helps in the creation of new memories. Chronic stress and anxiety also lead to increased production of glutamate in the brain – a neurotransmitter that causes migraine, and also depression when it is produced in excess amount.

It is the inability of the vagus nerve to activate the parasympathetic rest and digest response when stressed or anxious that keeps the sympathetic nervous system up and running, thus making us respond with impulse and end up suffering from the effect.

Trauma, PTSD, and Depression

Witnessing a traumatic event such as natural disasters, an act of violence, abuse, or even a severe accident can affect one's mental wellbeing, which can lead to mental disorders. Whether we are directly involved in such incidents, or we have family or friends that were affected (killed or injured), or even learning of the incident through the media, we will still experience some level of emotional response. Irrespective of the nature of the trauma, it can have a long-lasting psychological effect on an individual.

The feelings we experience from traumatic events (such as sadness, mood swings, crying, social withdrawal, etc.) are part of the normal grieving and recovery process from any trauma. However, if these feelings remain unchecked and continue quite too often for an extended period of time and it starts to affect your daily living, you begin to abuse alcohol or illegal drugs, or you even have the thoughts of suicide, then they are symptoms of a more severe episode of depression. Also, some people respond to their trauma by exhibiting post-traumatic stress disorder (PTSD) tendencies. When this occurs, they find themselves reliving repeated flashbacks of the traumatic event, continuous nightmares, inability to focus, and largely they remain miserable. Depression and PTSD are signs of an out of control trauma – they are all closely related to each other.

The vagus nerve is actively involved in your emotional wellbeing, and it determines how much you will be emotionally affected by a traumatic event long after it is has ended.

A reduced heart rate variability (HRV) is a potential pointer of an increased emotional sensitivity following a trauma, an indication of an altered vagus nerve function, and impaired emotion regulation ability. Through the vagus nerve, the HRV parasympathetic regulation of the heart rate is measured. During safe non-traumatic situations, the vagus nerve reduces your heart rate. However, when responding to threats, the inhibiting heart-rate effect of the vagus nerve stops, which then allows the sympathetic nervous system to activate defense responses and increasing your heart rate. Continuous exposure to threats could affect the functioning of the vagus nerve over time –resulting in a reduced capability of your body to adjust to traumatic events. High HRV is a marker that your body has an increased emotion regulation ability even after experiencing a traumatic or stressful event, while low HRV clearly indicates the opposite. Low HRV has been linked to increased exposure to trauma, PTSD, depression, and delayed recovery from a stressful situation.

Lack of Social Interaction

Maintaining face to face social interaction engages your vagus nerve and increases your parasympathetic response, which is very important for your health. Imagine being isolated from people or being indoor for a whole week or more without having to have a face to face interaction with the outside world, your family members, partners, or even your close friends; you would most certainly become somewhat low spirited and moody. This is not a random feeling – your vagus nerve activates when you interact with people face to face and deactivates when you are isolated. Social connectedness improves heart rate variability (HRV), an indication of a high vagal tone.

A study published in Health Psychology in 2009 showed that participants who exhibited signs of depression and were isolated from social interactions had a low HRV. However, when they were engaged in face to face interactions with their partners, friends, or family members, their vagal parasympathetic response and HRV increased. This goes to demonstrate that having a face to face social interaction would improve the functioning of your vagus nerve while a lack of social interaction points to an underperforming vagus nerve.

Sleep Disorders and Disruptive Circadian Rhythm

A very common problem I have observed among people is an alteration of their body's natural sleep signaling or their circadian rhythm. The reason for this is partly because most people do not engage in more bodily activity during the day. A common routine during the day, for instance, would be to take the subway or drive our car to work, sit on our work desk for an extended number of hours, and at the close of work, we take the subway or drive our car back home.

Hardly do we see the sun during our time of work, and when we get back to our homes, we sit right in front of blue lights at night e.g., our mobile phones, computers or even our television – these blue lights falsely telling our brains that it is daytime. These blue light that is emitted from the screen of our electronic devices mimics the sun, tells our bodies it is time to get up, and instructs the pineal glands in our brains not to release melatonin (hormone promoting sleep).

Signals are transmitted by the vagus nerve from our circadian control center, which is high up in our brain. Disrupting the circadian flow affects the brain, and alterations in melatonin and any other hormone levels right before bedtime can result in problems with the vagus nerve.

Chronic Inflammation

If you have been following this book from the get-go, then you should know that I made it clear that a certain amount of inflammation after an injury or infection is not out of place, especially if it occurs temporarily. The sympathetic nervous system swiftly dives into action by triggering your body's immune system to respond immediately.

Inflammation is simply indicating your body's immune system is prepared to protect you from further harm so that you can heal. When inflammation occurs, blood vessels around the location of the injury or infection expands, releasing more immune system cells into the tissue surrounding the affected area. Temporal redness, swelling, and pain accompany the inflammation process – at this point, you have nothing to really worry about, so just relax, you are experiencing what is called acute inflammation.

Immediately your immune system reacts to the injury or infection by protecting it from further harm, the process of healing becomes activated by your parasympathetic nervous system in other for your body to relax and restore balance. Stress caused by the injury or infection becomes reduced, your heart and breathing rates revert to the status quo, and the inflammation starts to dissipate. However, if the parasympathetic nervous system is not functioning properly, your heart and breathing rates could remain high, and the inflammation can stay back to become chronic, paving the way to severe health problems such as rheumatoid arthritis or lupus among others – now this is where you should be worried, and very concerned, and obviously, our aim is to ensure it does not get to this point.

You must now, by now, that the vagus nerve is directly tied to your parasympathetic nervous system because of the important role it plays in stress reduction, lowering of high heart and breathing rates, and preventing any acute inflammation from being chronic. It also resets your immune system, preventing it from overreacting and over-responding, especially when there is no need to. If the vagus nerve is not in a healthy state, it can't counterbalance your sympathetic nervous system nor reset your immune system, which can result in a list of health conditions affiliated with chronic inflammation. Hence, keeping your vagus nerve in good and healthy condition is vital to your overall health and wellbeing, which can help protect you from the health problems that come with chronic inflammation.

Dysfunctional Breathing

Most of us unknowingly take our breathing for granted due to "how we breathe" as opposed to "how we should breathe."

What if I told you that you have dysfunctional breathing?

One of the most common reasons for vagus nerve missignaling is dysfunctional breathing.

When we were babies, we learned how to breathe automatically through the proper way i.e., using the diaphragm to breathe – this is known as belly breathing or abdominal breathing, a process of using the primary muscles (such as diaphragm muscle) to breathe normally instead of the secondary muscles (used for heavy breathing). As we inhale, our diaphragm contracts, pulls down, and decreases the pressure in our chest, and as we exhale, it relaxes and causes us to breathe out with our belly expanding in the process. This process of breathing helps our lungs to inflate very efficiently, allows the exchange of important oxygen and nutrients, as well as the removal of waste products. Interestingly when you breathe using your diaphragm, you are inadvertently activating your parasympathetic nervous system, through the signals of your vagus nerve, allowing your body to slow down, and heal during tense situations which are accompanied by reduced heart rate and blood pressure, relaxed muscles, improved digestion, decreased stress, increased energy levels, and mood elevation among others.

However, as we get older, our breathing becomes shallower (chest breathing) as we begin to use our secondary muscles (such as neck muscles, muscles between our ribs, and our chest muscles), which can cause pains in our neck, shoulder and severe headaches from overactive muscles. This process of breathing does not allow your lungs to inflate nor deflate properly, prevents the circulation of important nutrients and oxygen, as well as causing retention of more waste products in your body. Breathing with your chest for a long while could decrease how well your body responds to infection and disease, exerts more pressure on your heart, and makes fighting respiratory conditions more difficult. Chest breathing in contrast to diaphragm breathing activates your sympathetic nervous system, which raises your heart rate and blood pressure, increases the tension in your muscles, increases stress, and decreases your energy and mental clarity. When your body is subjected to stress for a long period of time, your immune system risks being inefficient, and as time passes by, the build-up of minor irritations can result in issues like anxiety, depression, and constant illness and infections.

Breathing properly is one of the simplest things to do for your health, but yet seen as very challenging by many. In subsequent sections where I focused on how to strengthen your vagal tone, I would describe how you can learn to breathe properly for a better and healthy living.

Dysfunctional Digestive System

Right off the bat, when the vagus nerve is dysfunctional, your digestion system stands the risk of being dysfunctional. Some of the signs of a dysfunctional digestion system may include heartburn or gastroesophageal reflux disease (GERD), and inflammatory bowel disease (IBD) such as ulcerative colitis which can prevent your body from healing small intestine bacterial overgrowth (SIBO), a common cause of irritable bowel syndrome (IBS).

The vagus nerve tells your stomach to release digestive acids and enzymes and to begin the gut movement. When you chew your food, you begin the process of mixing the fibers in your food with the digestive acids and enzymes which start to breakdown the food before it gets to your stomach and before traveling down to your small and large intestines.

When the vagus nerve is not receiving or transmitting the right signals, the flow of food mixed with digestive acid and enzymes via the gut is slowed. The implication of this is that bacteria overgrowths, yeast or parasite, including used up hormones and toxins your body worked to remove from your body system, are traveling through your gut at a slow rate. Your body's exposure to these bacteria increases the risk of having IBS and SIBO, which can potentially worsen any infections already present in your body.

Dysfunctional Heart Rate

The number of times the heart beats per minute is referred to as the heart rate, and it is directly associated with the workload the heart is subjected to as we go about our daily life activities.

When the body is at rest (i.e., relaxed for a given amount of time), the resting heart rate can be measured. The normal resting heart rate for most people falls within the range of 60-100 beats per minute (bpm). However, for athletics, it is normal if it falls within 40-60 bpm. Dysfunctional heart rate or abnormal heart rhythms describes a heart that is beating too fast (above 100 bpm) or too slow (below 60 bpm).

The electrical signals of the sympathetic nervous system control the heart rate and release the hormones (epinephrine and norepinephrine) to increase the heart rate, while the parasympathetic nervous system causes the release of acetylcholine hormone through the vagus nerve to reduce the heart rate. In other words, the strength of your vagus nerve is determined by how low your resting heart rate is. Factors such as stress, excitement, or even exercising may elevate your heart rate temporarily while engaging in deep breaths, or meditation, for instance, can help slow your heart rate. When your heartbeat is unable to revert to its normal resting heart rate after a stressful event or activity, then this may be a pointer of a dysfunctional vagus nerve. When you are able to calm your nerves and slow down your heart after stress, then it is a marker you have a strong vagus nerve. The opposite is someone with a dysfunctional vagus nerve. An abnormally low heart rate (called bradycardia) can also occur if the vagus nerve is overactive. Bradycardia is when the resting heart rate is below 60 beats per minute, which is healthy and normal, especially for athletics, whose resting heart rate ranges from 40-60, as earlier mentioned. However, problems can be caused by bradycardia if the heart rate is so low that the heart cannot pump enough blood to supply the needs of the body. How well you are able to handle stressful situations would determine how well your vagus nerve would respond. If you are unable to function in a stressful situation, then an overactive vagus nerve can also occur. This makes sense especially if stress is over-activated causing your body to over-activate your vagus nerve i.e., a lot of chemicals slowing your heart rate and lowering your blood pressure, which means less blood circulation to the brain, making you lose consciousness momentarily, and causing you to faint – a term known as vasovagal syncope. Although vasovagal syncope is a sign of improper balance within the autonomic nervous system (i.e., between the sympathetic and parasympathetic nervous system), the imbalance is, however, not the single cause. Different causes exist and vary between young and old individuals. Vasovagal syncope is not life-threatening except someone faints quite too often, and if that is the case, it is often a sign of an immune issue that is yet to be diagnosed. Conducting a functional lab test and neurology can shed more light on the potential root cause, which is, in most cases, a symptom that the nerves in the autonomic nervous system and overactivation of the vagus nerve are not functioning properly.

Chapter 4

Substances That May Affect Your Vagus Nerve

While it is important for you to recognize certain factors that could interfere with the healthy functioning of your vagus nerve such as stress, anxiety, smoking, alcoholism, and poor sleeping habits among others, you should also keep watch of certain chemical substances that enters your body aside from the food you eat. You will be shocked that some of the substances you presumed to be unharmful can potentially cause severe damage to your vagus nerve.

Let's have a look at some of these substances.

Botox

It is a known fact that Botox (botulinum toxin) has several vital medical applications, and prominent amongst them is its usage in reducing lines and facial wrinkles by paralyzing the underlying muscles. Although Botox is applied in the treatment of some medical conditions, you should also be aware that it is a powerful and dangerous toxin which, when used inappropriately, can result in Botulism, an illness that causes respiratory failure, and eventually lead to death. A study shows that a gram of botulinum toxin has the capacity to kill over a million people, and two kilograms could potentially exterminate the entire human population – this is how dangerous it is.

So then, how can Botox cause damage to your vagus nerve?

When Botox is injected into the body, one of its targets is to stop the production of the chemical neurotransmitter called acetylcholine. Acetylcholine production is stimulated by the vagus nerve, which, when released, causes our muscles to contract, regulates our endocrine system, and aids in learning and memory formation, among others. When the vagus nerve does not stimulate the release of acetylcholine, our nerves will fail to receive signals, which would result in some problems such as myasthenia gravis, a disorder that affects the voluntary muscle contraction of the face, neck, mouth, and eyes. Sufferers of this disorder would have difficulty breathing, swallowing, and speaking. Other problems that may arise are double vision, and droopy eyelids.

As you can see, Botox has far too severe consequences when used wrongly. Can you imagine not being able to breathe or swallow? This can either lead to death or problems with some of your vital organs.

In using Botox, you should be well educated on the risks it has to your health. Should you decided to further its usage in treating any medical condition, ensure to choose an experienced and certified doctor to perform the Botox procedure, and also adhere to the doctor's instructions after the surgery.

Certain Antibiotics

There appears to be a thin line between certain antibiotics, most especially fluoroquinolone and its effect on the vagus nerve. Unfortunately, not enough research has been conducted and released on how fluoroquinolones can impact the vagus nerve.

However, I would provide you with my perspective on this.

Fluoroquinolones (ciprofloxacin, levofloxacin, moxifloxacin, and its other brands) are antibiotics used commonly in the treatment of several bacteria-related illnesses, most especially, respiratory and urinary tract infections. The FDA in 2013 strengthened its warning that fluoroquinolones could cause severe and permanent nerve damage called peripheral neuropathy and required updates to drug labels to reflect this risk.

Peripheral neuropathy arises when nerves are damaged and unable to send signals from the brain and spinal cord to the muscles and other parts of the body. It would interest you to know that the autonomic nervous system, risk being damaged by fluoroquinolone antibiotics.

Having established that peripheral neuropathy causes damage to the nerves, and given our knowledge that the vagus nerve is the longest of all 12 nerves that connect to multiple organs in our body from the brain and that this same nerve is part of the autonomic nervous system, there is no doubt that fluoroquinolones can cause damage to the vagus nerve. You might disapprove of my conclusion from this theory due to lack of adequate facts and data, but personally, I know this because once when I had a severe reaction to ciprofloxacin, each of those body functions controlled by the vagus nerve was affected.

Though no scientific evidence is yet to be published in support of this theory, my interactions with several patients that experienced similar symptoms prove this theory is valid. It took the FDA about 30 years to recognize the effect of fluoroquinolones, so I would not be swift to disregard its possible effect on the autonomic nervous system and, by extension, its effect on the vagus nerve. I suspect the reason the FDA has not investigated the autonomic neuropathy's possible association with fluoroquinolones is because the problems that arise from the autonomic nervous system are difficult to describe and detect, but most importantly, it hasn't gotten to the top list of complaints in the AERS database (where FDA receives medication error complaints and reports).

Research also shows that administering fluoroquinolones to patients with a history of myasthenia gravis (earlier discussed) can exacerbate this disorder, and can lead to death. Hence, administering fluoroquinolone antibiotics to such patients should be avoided.

This by no means implies that fluoroquinolone antibiotics should not be administered when the need arises, but it should be used in addition to probiotics, which is used to add vital bacteria into the body, which the fluoroquinolone antibiotics may have removed. Nonetheless, always consult with your doctor and be well educated on the risks of using fluoroquinolones.

Heavy Metals

Heavy metals such as arsenic, cadmium, copper, iron, lead, mercury, and zinc, among others, are all around us. They can be found in the food we eat, the water we drink, the ground we walk on, the injections we receive into our body, and in our everyday cosmetic care products, to say the least. Not all of these metals are toxic to our bodies. For instance, our bodies require a small amount of copper, zinc, and iron to perform some physiological and biological activities in order to keep us healthy. High amounts of heavy metals, in general, can have a severe impact on our health, which can damage and disrupt the functioning of our internal organs such as the kidney, lungs, and liver, to mention but a few. Of all the heavy metals, mercury poses the most threat to our body.

How then does mercury affect the vagus nerve?

Just like Botox, which inhibits the production of acetylcholine, research also validates the same for mercury. Mercury prevents the action of acetylcholine. For instance, when mercury finds its way to the heart muscle receptors, the heart muscle would be unable to receive the vagus nerve electrical signal needed for contraction. The implication of this could result in cardiovascular problems such as cardiac arrest.

It is important to get in touch with your doctor to test for the amount of mercury in your body. If your body has a high amount of mercury, request to undergo a mercury detox. Although trace amounts of mercury can be found in the food we eat, which our body can control, you should take additional steps to minimize your exposure to high mercury. Some of which are but not limited to the following:

- Avoiding fishes with high mercury such as tuna and swordfish
- Avoiding amalgam fillings
- Avoiding skin-lightening products and other cosmetics with high mercury concentration
- Using water filters that are designed to filter mercury

- Wearing gloves when digging the soil of your gardens to limit the absorption of mercury into your skin

Excess Sugar Intake

Some foods, like sugar, can also cause inflammation in the body, which is normal. However, taking excess added sugar poses severe health risks, such as high blood pressure and diabetes – a disease characterized by an increased blood sugar level, which potentially leads to the damage of the blood vessels, heart, kidneys, and nerves. Unfortunately, high blood pressure and diabetes are not the only concern that poses a risk to the human body; chronic inflammation can also result from the intake of excess added sugar. Don't get me wrong, inflammation is a normal part of our body's healing process in which some sugar-laden foods could cause, which is very normal. However, consuming excess sugar (added sugar and not natural sugar) that goes unchecked could result in chronic inflammation, which is the root cause of many chronic diseases. These inflammations can likewise disrupt the body's nervous systems from signaling information across different parts of the body.

Preventing interruptions to our body's communication system is thus vital to the healthy functioning of the body, which is why you should be careful enough to watch the amount of added sugar you allow into your body.

Being watchful of the substances mentioned herein and adhering to the do's and don'ts are a vital part of ensuring your vagus nerve is not damaged but alive and kicking. That being said, you could potentially slip and fall victim to these substances, which could cause severe damage to your vagus nerve. It is important to note that these substances are only a few of what could cause damage to your vagus nerve. Other factors, as discussed throughout this book, can also contribute to the malfunctioning of your vagus nerve. This is the more reason why you need to be well informed on how to stimulate the vagus nerve to fight against the health problems that may arise from either these substances or the other factors already discussed.

How you can stimulate this nerve is our focus for the next chapter.

The end... almost!

Hey! We've made it to the final chapter of this book, and I hope you've enjoyed it so far.

If you have not done so yet, I would be incredibly thankful if you could take just a minute to leave a quick review on the product page of this book.

Reviews are not easy to come by, and as an independent author with a little marketing budget, I rely on you, my readers, to leave a short review on the product page of this book

Even if it is just a sentence or two!

So if you really enjoyed this book, please... leave a brief review on the product page of this book.

I truly appreciate your effort to leave your review, as it truly makes a huge difference.

Thanks once again from the depth of my heart for purchasing this book and reading it to the end.

Chapter 5

Stimulating Your Vagus Nerve

When you develop a deep understanding of how your vagus nerve works, you will find it possible to work with your nervous system instead of feeling trapped when it works against you. It wouldn't be out of place to mention that I have enjoyed a sound physical and mental health over the years (which I still do), simply because I understood the incredible effect stimulating my vagus nerve had on my overall wellbeing.

Throughout the course of this book, I shed several lights on the anatomy of the vagus nerve, its importance to your physical and mental wellbeing, the causes of an impaired vagus nerve, the health conditions associated with it, and why it is important to increase the tone and strength of your vagus nerve. In this chapter, I would reveal in detail what you should do to increase the tone of your vagus nerve vis-a-vis engaging in specific natural exercises and practices, passive methods of stimulation, as well as recommended food and dietary supplements. Be aware that some of these methods may seem offbeat, but what I am about to reveal are based on science and are all found to be very effective at increasing your vagal tone.

Without further ado, let's dive in.

Natural Exercises and Practices

Deep and Slow Breathing

Earlier, I discussed the effect of dysfunctional breathing mostly because we breathe through our chest instead of our diaphragm. In this section, I would be describing how you can start breathing the proper way using the deep and slow diaphragmatic breathing technique.

But before then...

Many of us don't breathe properly while at rest, we breathe at a very fast pace (about 10-14 breaths per minute instead of taking about 5-7 breaths per minute). When this happens, we short change ourselves from the power the vagus nerve has on our wellbeing. When you take a deep, slow breath, your vagus nerve becomes stimulated by lowering your sympathetic (fight or flight) nervous system and activating your parasympathetic (rest and digest) nervous system. When this happens, your heart rate, blood pressure, and any feelings of anxiety become reduced.

Deep and slow breathing exercises can also help divert your attention away from the sensation of pain.

How do I mean?

If you focus your attention on the rhythm of your breathing, you won't feel the sensation of your pain since you are not focused on the pain itself. On the flip side, when you focus on the pain, you will be forced to hold our breath. Anytime you hold your breath, the fight or flight response gets activated, which then increases not just the sensation of pain but also sensations of stiffness, fear, and anxiety. To practice deep and slow breathing, you must learn to breathe through your diaphragm and not through your chest – this drains your energy and makes you anxious, among others.

To start breathing from your diaphragm, proceed as follows:

- Get comfortable by either sitting on a chair while resting your head, neck, and shoulders against the back of the chair or laying your back against the floor or bed, supported by a pillow to your head and feet.
- Lay one of your hand on your upper chest and the other on your belly.

- Shut your eyes and breathe in deeply and slowly into your belly via your nose (i.e., to expand your diaphragm) to the count of five, take a pause then

- Slowly exhale through your mouth to the count of ten

- Repeat the same process for about 5-10 minutes

Ideally, your breath has to be reduced to 5-7 breaths per minute to activate the parasympathetic rest and digest mode. As your breath per minute is reduced and the parasympathetic mode gets activated, your muscles become relaxed, causing all sensations of pain, fear, anxiety, or even worries to be lowered. When this happens, the supply of oxygen to the cells of your body increases which then help to produce your body's feel-good hormones called endorphins.

You can enhance your breathing experience as you inhale while imagining the beauty of being loved or the air being filled with peace and calm, and as you exhale, imagine reciprocating that same love or the air leaving with any sensations of pain, or anxiety. There is nothing really mysterious about this breathing technique. This is an ancient technique that has been practiced for decades by the Tibetan monks, which can also help improve your memory, tackle depression, as well as boost your immune system – at a price of zero dollars.

How often you decide to practice this breathing technique solely depends on you. You can either make it a daily routine or anytime you feel on edge. However, I recommend the former so that you not only train yourself to stop breathing through your chest but also be able to easily adapt to the breathing technique, making it more easy to initiate whenever you are on edge. Practicing deep, slow, and diaphragmatic breathing to activate your vagus nerve can perform wonders for your physical and mental wellbeing.

Humming or Chanting

The vagus nerve fibers originating from the brainstem connects your larynx (voice box) and the muscles behind your throat, and it is responsible for governing the movement of your vocal cords. As a matter of fact, impairment of the vagus nerve is what causes vocal paralysis. Humming or chanting have been proven to stimulate the vagus nerve, and awakening the laryngeal muscles, thereby increasing the vagal tone. A study performed by Dr. Stephen Porges showed that the vibrations produced from humming or chanting aloud wake up your vagus nerve so that it comes online. To begin stimulating your vagus nerve through this practice, all you need to do is chant the word "OM," "home," "hum," or "hmmm," while stretching the "mmm" sound for as long as possible (say 10 secs or more). You can observe and enjoy the vibration sensations produced in your head, chest, throat, ear, and even throughout your body. Continue humming or chanting for about 10-15 minutes per session, with up to 2 sessions in a day or as many as you can perform per day.

This exercise is most productive when performed on a daily basis. Humming or chanting affords us the ability to regulate our breath and calm down our thoughts, especially during or after a stressful event. It is also shown to improve the level of digestion and inflammation in the body.

Singing

Just like humming or chanting, singing also activates the vagus nerve and awakens the laryngeal muscles. Singing is like activating a vagal pump to send out waves of relaxation. I usually sing my favorite songs at the top of my voice anytime I feel moody, and a surge of positive energy immediately flows through my body, calming my frayed nerves. It does not matter whether you choose to sing alone or in unison (in a church or with a group of friends), either of such would activate the vagus nerve function, increase relaxation and elevate your mood, and also increase your heart rate variability (HRV).

Humor Therapy

Laughing is one very easy way to stimulate the vagus nerve. It is a natural immune booster to the body, which, by research, is also found to increase one's heart rate variability (HRV). Laughing increases the movement of your diaphragm and the pressure on your abdomen (stomach). Because the vagus nerve travels from the brainstem, passing through the diaphragm, these movements would activate your rest and digest the parasympathetic nervous system that sends signals to your body to relax. When you laugh, you are typically activating your rest and digest the nervous system to lower your stress hormones and trigger the release of the body's painkillers, such as endorphins (a feel-good hormone). Stepping out for a comedy show, watching a comedy film, or simply joking around with families and friends is one sure way to get started. However, you don't necessarily need to laugh aloud to have a feel of the soothing relief laughter can bring when your vagus nerve is stimulated. You can also find something in your office that can make you smile, watch a humorous television program, read humorous books or anything that makes you chuckle on the inside – all are just as therapeutic as laughing out loud.

Gargling

The gargling technique was popularized by Dr. Datis Kharrazian, which simply means holding and pouring a liquid (i.e., water) into the mouth, and to the back of the throat while moving it around aggressively to make a gurgling sound.

When you gargle, the pharyngeal muscles (muscles at the back of your throat) contracts, causing the activation of your vagus nerve – it is often described as "sprints" for your vagus nerve. For gargling to be effective, you would need to gargle aggressively and loudly, to the point where tears come into your eyes, and if it doesn't, keep going at it until you do. This actually shows that you have activated your vagus nerve. This can be pretty difficult to do at first, especially if your vagal tone is weak. Ideally, you should be gargling for up to 5 minutes, three times per day. However, start with a shorter time and build up gradually. Adding salt to the water when you are about to gargle has been shown to produce an anti-bacteria impact that can help eliminate unwanted bacteria from the mouth and respiratory tract.

Gargling on a daily basis would help increase your vagus nerve responsiveness to regulate relaxation, metabolism, and digestion, and it has also been demonstrated to improve memory performance.

Gag Reflex

Gag reflex, just like gargling, is another way to stimulate the pharyngeal muscles that the vagus nerve innervates, and is often described as "push-ups" for your vagus nerve. Gag reflex (also called pharyngeal reflex) occurs when the back of your tongue or even the roof of your mouth is touched by an object that causes the back of your throat to contract. Gag reflex helps protect us from choking as well as helping to govern the transition of food from liquid to solid during infancy. You can use a tongue depressor, your toothbrush, or any convenient but safe object to activate the gag reflex. Ideally, for this exercise to produce the much-needed change such as increasing your vagal tone, it should be done several times (i.e., 5-10) on a daily basis, spanning several weeks and mostly importantly it should be done until tear comes into your eyes (a sign that your vagus nerve has been stimulated). As a precautionary measure, gently press whatever object you choose to use on the back of your tongue, then push down gradually to the back of your throat to activate the gag reflex. This is to prevent you from poking the back of your throat with the object and hurting yourself. Activating the gag reflex immediately fires up the vagus nerve to keep sending signals that the body requires.

Exposure to Cold

Cold exposure has been described to activate the vagus nerve. Studies show that when you regularly expose your body to cold, your body adjusts to the cold, causing a decrease in the activity of the fight or flight nervous system while increasing the rest and digest nervous system activity.

Immersion of the face in cold water proves to be a simple but yet effective way to activate the parasympathetic nervous system after a stressful activity such as an exercise or when you generally feel worn out. For the cold water face immersion to be very effective, it is recommended that you remain seated, bending your head forward into a cold water basin at a temperature of about 10-12°C. Your face should be immersed such that your forehead, your eyes, and two-thirds of your cheeks are also submerged in the water.

Coldwater showers can also be taken, likewise finishing your warm water shower with at 30 seconds or more of cold water. Alternatively, you can put some cubes of ice in a sealed bag, and then hold it up against your face, while holding your breath for some time, or you can take a swim in a cold water pool - these are all great ways to get your vagus nerve online.

I have experimented with all these techniques, and I have found them to be quite exhilarating. Often times, I take cold showers and go outside, especially when the temperature is cold, with minimal clothing. If you reside in a cold winter climate area, then it would be great if you could take a walkout on a frigid day. Otherwise, try using cold therapy in a cryo-chamber (a tank of the size of a human, filled with nitrogen-cooled air) if you can afford it – the majority of athletes and performers such as Tony Robbins uses this method.

These methods, as described, can easily stimulate an unresponsive vagus nerve when done regularly, helping to reduce your heart rate, blood pressure, and lowering your stress hormone levels – overall boosting your immune system.

Sudarshan Kriya Yoga

As shown by research, yoga (a mind-body relaxation practice) can stimulate the vagus nerve by elevating your parasympathetic activity and reducing inappropriate activation of your autonomic activity. A clinical trial conducted on irritable bowel syndrome (IBS) patients showed that the overactivation of the sympathetic nervous system was the main contributing cause of the disease. Yoga, which increases the parasympathetic activity of the nervous system, proved to be a remedial therapy for IBS.

The sudarshan kriya, asana, pranayama, and nadi shodhana yoga has been found by scientists to be extremely effective at stimulating the vagus nerve. However, one popular yoga technique shown to be very effective and scientifically proven to stimulate the vagus nerve naturally is the sudarshan kriya Yoga, a type of mind-body relaxation breathing technique. This technique harmonizes the body, the mind, and emotions through specific breathing rhythms to diffuse stress, fatigue, as well as negative emotions such as anger, depression, and frustration. In a scientific study conducted, it was shown that a 68%–73% success rate was recorded in its treatment of depression, and also shown to help treat people with PTSD. Another study showed that practicing sudarshan kriya led to a significant drop in cortisol levels (stress hormone), suggesting that continuous practice of this yoga technique would result in a greater level of stress resistance and relaxation.

Generally, practicing sudarshan kriya yoga increases the GABA level (a calming neurotransmitter in the brain that inhibits stress, anxiety, and mood swings) by directly stimulating vagal afferent fibers, which in turn increases the parasympathetic nervous system activity—making it very helpful for people who struggle with anxiety, depression, and PTSD.

Loving Kindness Meditation

Loving-kindness meditation has been shown to be very effective in stimulating the vagus nerve and increasing heart rate variability. Loving-kindness meditation helps people look beyond themselves and become more aware of others by promoting a feeling of goodwill toward their needs, struggles, and desires.

To practice loving-kindness meditation, you are required to sit in silence for a given amount of time while cultivating feelings of warmth, tenderness, and compassion toward others by silently repeating phrases to yourself that is aimed at wishing them love, strength, and general wellbeing. A study conducted in 2010 by

Barbara Fredrickson, a foremost researcher of positive emotions, showed that an increased positive emotion resulted in increased social closeness and a high vagal tone. And since social connection and bonds are mediated by vagal tone, those whose vagal tone increased were suddenly able to experience more moments of love toward others in subsequent times.

Regular practicing of loving-kindness meditation increases one's capacity to love even more, which can also translate into better health given that high vagal tone is associated with reduced risk of inflammation, cardiovascular disease, stroke, and even better mood among others.

Exposure to Sunlight

Sunlight exposure affects the cellular functioning of our body, which is genetically wired to function based on how much sunlight we are exposed to. When you spend your whole day away from the sun whether commuting to work via subways, or driving to work, or anywhere for that matter, and then returning home late in the evening from your busy work or activity without having enough skin to eye contact with the sun, you are more often depriving your cells from performing optimally.

Exposing your eye and skin to the sun is all about your circadian rhythm and having a good restful sleep at night. For instance, when light comes in contact with your eye (I don't mean looking directly into the sun), the melanopsin protein in the retina detects the light using vitamin A, and then it signals the brain that it is day time. But when it is nightfall, this signal is then turned off. Studies show that when you expose your eye and skin to sunlight, the melatonin (sleep hormone) levels increase at night.

Exposure to sunlight is linked to boosting serotonin production in the brain, and also facilitates your circadian rhythm and vagus nerve to regulate your heart rate. Hence, it is recommended that you go outside more often on a sunny day to feel the sun's warmth.

Precaution, however, should be taken when exposed to sunlight because having too much of the sun's rays (UVA and UVB) can be harmful to you. Instead, you should strike a balance between these rays. UVA and UVB rays are strongest between 10 a.m and 4 p.m, therefore the best times for sunlight exposure should be within 30 minutes of sunrise (2-3 times in the day) and 30 minutes of sunset.

Coffee Enema

A coffee enema is basically used for detoxification and gut motility, i.e., to cleanse your bowels and relieve constipation. When you take a coffee enema, the caffeine it contains will stimulate the release of the cholinergic receptor (in particular, the nicotinic receptor) in the gut, which then stimulates the movement and expansion of your bowel, thus activating your vagus nerve. This is particularly effective if high concentration of caffeine is taken, which then creates the urge to have a bowel movement. The key is to resist the urge and try holding it for as long as possible. By resisting the urge, you are actually training your brain and vagus nerve to learn how to activate your gut motility. If you do this regularly with a coffee enema, after a while, your vagus nerve would have learned how to release stools from your bowel without depending on coffee enema. At first, it may be difficult to keep up with, especially if your vagal tone is low, but with time, it becomes easier. If you suffer from chronic constipation and poor liver detoxification, there is no doubt that the process of taking coffee enema and resisting the urge would help detoxify your body and clear out your bowels very efficiently.

Personally, I used coffee enema on a daily basis for several months when I underwent an intensive program for detoxification while also resisting the urge. Over time, it helped me wean off any dependency on them, thus enabling my vagus nerve to activate my gut motility and restoring healthy bowel movements when I needed to detoxify and cleanse my bowels.

Overall, when it comes to your health, most especially the health of your gut, nothing is more critical than attending to your brain health and stimulating your vagal nerve response. By doing so, your gastrointestinal motility can be improved, thereby eliminating constipation and poor detoxification.

Massage

Having a massage is another way to stimulate your vagus nerve. I always visit the spa every weekend for some massage treatment, especially after a very stressful weekday just to destress my body, and the feeling afterward is always soothing and invigorating. Getting a massage instantly makes you relaxed, and when you are relaxed, your parasympathetic rest and digest response gets triggered. Anytime you activate your parasympathetic nervous system, you inadvertently stimulate your vagus nerve.

Massaging several areas of your body, most especially along your carotid artery (the side of your neck where a pulse is checked) or your foot is highly efficient for vagus nerve stimulation. A study shows that massage done to the throat region are found to reduce seizures while foot massages when performed can be helpful to increase your heart rate variability (HRV) and vagal activity, while also reducing your heart rate and blood pressure, all of which minimizes the risk of heart diseases. If you have never gone to the spa to get a massage, I strongly recommend that you do, but if you are not financially buoyant to visit the spa, you can do so at the comfort of your home. Your spouse, partner, or someone you are comfortable with can help massage your foot. However, doing a carotid artery massage at home by an unprofessional is not recommended because it could possibly lead to fainting.

Movement or Exercise

Most brain health professionals recommend movement or exercise as their top piece of advice for maximum brain health functioning. Exercise has been found to stimulate the vagus nerve which then helps increase the brain's growth hormone, supports the brain's energy as well as help reverse cognitive decline – which clearly points to the positive effects it has on our brain and overall mental health. Many of us do not put our bodies to work, with no actual movement or exercise to warm up our bodies. Most times, we are in a fixed spot, sitting for long periods at work, in the car, on the couch at home, or any other place for that matter without really moving or exercising our body for a good amount of time. Its high time you started a routine of movement or exercise that increases your heart rate and, by so doing, improves your parasympathetic rest and digest system, as well as training your body to easily recover from stress.

To get started, you can choose whatever movement or exercise that works best for you. Walking, weightlifting and sprinting are some of the best exercises you can start with. However, it is recommended that you choose an exercise or sporting activity that you love and enjoy to enable you to keep at it consistently.

Here is my exercise routine:

- Heavy weightlifting (4 times per week)
- High-intensity sprinting (2 times per week)
- Walking every day for 30-60 minutes

Food and Dietary Supplement

Probiotics

Earlier in this book, I discussed how the vagus nerve facilitates communication between our gut and the brain, and the role the microbiome (bacteria) in our gut plays with regard to our physical and mental health. The healthy bacteria present in our gut are what stimulates the positive feedback loop to our brain via the Vagus nerve. What I mean to say is that these bacteria in our gut basically stimulates the release of various neurotransmitters (such as Serotonin, Dopamine, and GABA, which are partly responsible for how we feel and what we think) to our brain, and mediated by the vagus nerve. Our body has lots of bacteria, both those that are good and those that are bad. Probiotics are live microorganisms (usually bacteria) that are found in food or supplements and are intended to reproduce, maintain and or improve the healthiness of the good bacteria in our body such as that found in our gut.

Lactobacillus Rhamnosus and Bifidobacterium Longum are the two main species that the majority of probiotic supplements are made of. For instance, research showed that probiotics stimulate the production of important neurotransmitters that impacts our mental health, and Lactobacillus Rhamnosus is one such probiotic, which was found to improve the Gamma-Aminobutyric Acid (GABA) neurotransmitter levels in the brain. It was found that the vagus nerve was stimulated by this probiotic bacteria, which in turn, stimulated the production of GABA. GABA has several functions it performs in the body, among which is to control anxiety and improve our mood. Bifidobacterium Longum also showed to normalize anxiety-like behavior in a clinical test conducted.

The vagus nerve essentially reads the gut microbiome, initiating a response to regulate inflammation based on whether it detects pathogenic or non-pathogenic bacteria. Probiotics help the vagus nerve to fight off inflammation, and when the gut microbiome is overrun by pathogenic (bad) bacteria, the result is the creation of the breeding ground for inflammation.

It is important you test your gut microbiome to know how healthy your gut is and also to determine if there are sufficient levels of probiotics in your gut. Probiotics in the gut microbiome can have a positive health impact on your immune system, and other factors that may reduce your vagal tone.

Fermented foods such as yogurt, kefir, sauerkraut, cheese, kimchi, sauerkraut, kombucha, and miso are known to be rich in probiotics. So, you may want to incorporate these foods as part of your diet. Nonetheless, always consult a health practitioner who is familiar with probiotics before you start or stop the intake of any probiotic-based supplement or food.

Omega-3 Fatty Acids

Omega-3 fatty acids are essential fats our body requires, which the body itself cannot produce, but rather, gotten from foods that are high in omega 3 such as salmon fish, walnuts, flaxseed, soybean oil, and seaweed. There is a lot of negativity pertaining to fatty foods. However, we all need healthy fat diets for our mental health, but the source of the fats we consume also matter. Research show that when you consume omega 3 fatty acids (which are primarily found in fish, most especially, fatty fish, e.g., salmon), it turns on your parasympathetic mode, thereby increasing your vagal tone and activity. To bring a balance to our system, we need about three times the amount of omega-3 fatty acids else, the vagal tone of our vagus nerve would decline.

While taking eicosapentaenoic acid (EPA), a type of omega-3 fatty acid important for cellular function, also ensure to get enough docosahexaenoic acid (DHA) in your diet. This is because DHA accounts for about 90% of the omega-3 fats in our brain. Nonetheless, our body can only produce a little amount of DHA from other fatty acids; hence, it has to be consumed from food or supplement. So, make sure you have a good amount of fish, oil, nuts, and or seeds that are high in omega 3 in other to get a high-quality DHA to stimulate your vagus nerve.

DHA and EPA are the two key types of omega- 3 fatty acids. Fish diets that are rich in DHA and EPA are salmon, mackerel, seabass, oysters, shrimp, and sardines, while seaweed and algae are vegetable diets that also contain DHA and EPA.

If you are unable to meet your omega-3 dietary requirements, then you can benefit from taking omega-3 supplements. There are many types of omega-3 supplements rich in DHA and EPA that you can choose from, such as fish oil, cod liver oil, krill oil, and algae oil. Personally, I eat a lot of salmon fish, supplemented with krill oil, in order to get my parasympathetic mode stimulated. Both DHA and EPA can help reduce inflammation as well as the risk of chronic diseases, such as heart disease.

Omega-3 fatty acid has been shown to help overcome addiction, reverse decline in cognitive ability, and even help to repair leaky brain. It has also been shown to increase heart rate variability in obese children, making it all too important for impacting several aspects of our mental health and overall wellness.

Passive Methods of Stimulation

Auricular Acupuncture

Really and truly, I am a very big fan of auricular (ear) acupuncture, a form of ancient alternative medicine that involves the insertion of needles into specific points on the ear. As earlier discussed, the vagus nerve is sensitive to touch felt on the skin of the ear, especially the external parts and receives sensory information via its auricular branch. Using the auricular acupuncture technique can, therefore, send sensory information to the vagus nerve via the auricular branch, which, in turn, causes a stimulation of the vagus nerve. This has also been validated by research and has been shown to increase vagal activity and tone, as well as help in the treatment of depression, anxiety, epilepsy, and digestive disorders.

There has been a growing trend in recent times, where the vagus nerve can be stimulated by a transcutaneous (non-invasive) electrical device applied to the external part of the ear, which was found to increase the parasympathetic rest and digest response and reduce the sympathetic fight or flight response. A reported study (Addorisio et al., 2019) showed that using a transcutaneous electrical device applied to certain parts of the ear to stimulate the vagus nerve activated the rest and digest nervous system in a way that drastically reduced inflammation.

Auricular acupuncture and the surgically implanted vagus nerve stimulation devices (to be discussed shortly) both provide the same effect. So, if you want to avoid surgical implants that are not invasive, then I would recommend you go with acupuncture, which is what I would personally go for at any time.

On a lighter note, it was once reported that a man passed on from a very low heart rate after vagus nerve stimulation using acupuncture. In light of this, I strongly advise that you work with a certified acupuncture practitioner and also notify your doctor if you intend to see an acupuncturist.

Chiropractor Care

The healthiness of the vagus nerve is very important to chiropractors because the vagus nerve is intimately associated with the spine and upper neck. The role the spinal health plays in coordinating the health of the vagus nerve is very significant. If the positioning of the spine and its ability to move freely becomes altered, the information that travels along the spinal nerves become interrupted. This is particularly noticed when you sit for long hours at work, busy working with your computer and hardly moving around. The result is a sensation of pain, mostly at your back and neck.

For better activity of the vagus nerve, chiropractors ensure the spines are well aligned and move freely. For instance, a study shows that the manipulation of the spine of a patient with pain (from lack of movement) at the back and neck by a chiropractor significantly improved the activity of the vagus nerve, resulting in reduced blood pressure and high heart rate variability (HRV). However, to experience sustained improvements in blood pressure and HRV, I strongly recommended that regular chiropractic care be administered.

When in pain, chiropractic care can be a very effective method to increase your parasympathetic and vagus nerve activity.

Electrical Stimulation

Over the years, scientists have been exploring the influence of the nerve on the brain. One of the very complicated and interesting nerve they explored is the vagus nerve, and to explore the influence of this nerve on the brain and the body in general, they came up with electrical stimulation devices to stimulate the vagus nerve. The stimulation of this nerve by means of electrical energy is popularly referred to as vagus nerve stimulation (VNS), which has been proven to help treat people with epilepsy and treatment-resistant depression.

Vagus nerve stimulation is a medical treatment, and part of an increasingly popular field called bioelectronics which through the vagus nerve, makes use of tested clinically devices (surgically implanted on the chest wall with a wire running from it to the vagus nerve in the neck) to hack the body's nervous system by sending mild pulses of electrical energy to the brain. Depending on the specific needs of the patient, these mild pulses are sent at periodic intervals all through the day at an individualized dosage level of frequency and amplitude.

In 1997, the FDA approved the use of an implantable (and invasive) VNS to reduce the severity of epileptic seizures in epileptic patients that were unresponsive to medications. According to the Epilepsy Foundation, when VNS was administered to epileptic patients, it provided periodic stimulation to the vagus nerve, which in turn decreased, and or in rare cases, stopped the brain activity that caused the seizures. Researchers began noticing a range of unexpected but positive side effects in the administration of the VNS treatments to patients. For example, it was noticed that patients who had a reduction in epileptic seizures after being administered the VNS treatment also had a noticeable improvement in their moods. Not only that, but symptoms of depression became fewer, systemic inflammation lowered, and severe headaches were reportedly reduced. Officially in 2002, the initial observations made by researchers on how VNS aborted migraine headaches in patients with epilepsy were published in the paper, thereby giving rise to the possibility of using VNS in the treatment of migraine headaches.

In 2005, the FDA also approved the use of an implantable VNS to treat people with treatment-resistant depression and has also been found helpful in treating conditions such as bipolar disorder, anxiety disorders, and Alzheimer's disease.

Further medical applications in the use of VNS were reported. A study published in the Proceedings of the National Academy of Sciences (PNAS) in 2016, showed that vagus nerve stimulation using a bioelectronic device improved the condition of patients with rheumatoid arthritis, an inflammatory disease that is reported to have affected 1.3 million people in the US and costing billions of dollars to treat annually.

Surgically implanting a VNS device comes with some risks, some of which include difficulty swallowing, vocal cord paralysis, hoarseness, throat pain, headaches, cough, shortness of breath, prickling of the skin, and insomnia to mention but a few. Most people can tolerate these side effects and may lessen with time, but for but some people, the side effects could be bothersome in as much as the VNS device is implanted. Adjusting the electrical impulses is a great way to reduce these side effects. However, if they remain intolerable, the device can be shut down temporarily or permanently. Luckily, with the advancement of technology, other devices for electrical stimulation that are neither invasive nor require implantation have been developed and approved to serve certain types of conditions. In view of this, the FDA approved the use of the transcutaneous VNS device called gammaCore, for the treatment of migraines and cluster headaches in the US, which has also been cleared for use in Europe. The gammaCore is a hand-held VNS device that is administered by gently pressing the device against the neck to stimulate the vagus nerve. Another transcutaneous VNS device is the NEMOS system, a device which when applied to the ear, stimulates the vagus nerve. At this time, it has been cleared in the treatment of epilepsy and depression in Europe.

The use of VNS devices does not come cheap, which is why following through with the natural exercises and practices, food and diet supplements or other non-electrical passive methods earlier discussed would be a great way to activate your vagus nerve and still address the health conditions associated with the vagus nerve. Whatever treatment method you decide to use or if you decide to combine several methods (depending on your specific health issue), they are all effective means through which you can improve your health from conditions such as chronic inflammation, anxiety, depression, and epilepsy among others.

Conclusion

I'd like to thank you and congratulate you for transiting my lines from start to finish.

I hope this book was able to help you understand the different health conditions that can arise when your vagus nerve is damaged, and why it is very important that you be mindful of your lifestyle habits as well as the food and substances you allow into your body. And most importantly, I hope that you found the methods of vagus stimulation shared in this book to be quite useful to help you get started in stimulating your vagus nerve and taking charge of your health and wellbeing for good.

At this point, you are now better equipped to take control of your health. The next step is to apply your preferred method of stimulation, be it the active exercises and practice, passive methods, or even the food and diet supplement tips that I discussed in the previous chapter of this book. This book has shown you the unlimited potentials that you can unlock for your health when you stimulate your vagus nerve. So, I urge you to feel free to experiment which of these methods would work best for your needs and current health situation. Personally, increasing my vagal tone through the stimulation of my vagus nerve afforded me the ability to overcome anxiety and depression, and some other conditions I once suffered from. This has also helped me better manage similar conditions when they arise.

Finally, I want you to take personal responsibility for your health and wellbeing by incorporating the tips I have shared in this book into your daily life routine. As you regularly follow through with your preferred exercise and practice, tip or method, the more likely your vagus nerve becomes stimulated.

Remember…

"Knowing is not enough; we must apply. Willing is not enough; we must do" –Goethe.

I wish you the very best on your journey toward health and wellness!

References

The Vagus Nerve (CN X) - Course - Functions - TeachMeAnatomy. (2019, January 28). Retrieved from https://teachmeanatomy.info/head/cranial-nerves/vagus-nerve-cn-x/

Kenhub. (2020, February 27). Vagus nerve. Retrieved from https://www.kenhub.com/en/library/anatomy/the-vagus-nerve

Seymour, T. (2017, June 28). Everything you need to know about the vagus nerve. Retrieved from https://www.medicalnewstoday.com/articles/318128#What-is-the-vagus-nerve

9 Fascinating Facts About the Vagus Nerve. (2018, November 13). Retrieved from https://www.mentalfloss.com/article/65710/9-nervy-facts-about-vagus-nerve

Jayne, P. (2019, September 19). Penelope Jayne. Retrieved from https://www.globalrecharge.guru/vagus-nerve-the-body-mind-connection/

Leonard, J. (2019, May 28). 10 ways to improve gut health. Retrieved from https://www.medicalnewstoday.com/articles/325293

Dukovac, N. (2019, September 27). Vagal Nerve Tone, Heart Rate Variability and Chiropractic. Retrieved from https://www.adelaidefamilychiro.com/blog/vagal-tone-heart-rate-variability-and-chiropractic

Validation of the Apple Watch for Heart Rate Variability Measurements during Relax and Mental Stress in Healthy Subjects. (2018, August 1). Retrieved from https://www.ncbi.nlm.nih.gov/pmc/articles/PMC6111985/

Hack Your Vagus Nerve to Feel Better: 14 Easy Ways. (2019, August 12). Retrieved from https://victoriaalbina.com/vagusnerve/

Holland, K. (2019, April 18). Mercury Detox: Separating Fact from Fiction. Retrieved from https://www.healthline.com/health/mercury-detox#reducing-exposure

Harvard Health Publishing. (2019, November 5). The sweet danger of sugar. Retrieved from https://www.health.harvard.edu/heart-health/the-sweet-danger-of-sugar

GÁL, K. (2020, January 20). What are the best sources of omega-3? Retrieved from https://www.medicalnewstoday.com/articles/323144#omega-3-supplements

Harvard Health Publishing. (2019, November 5). The sweet danger of sugar. Retrieved from https://www.health.harvard.edu/heart-health/the-sweet-danger-of-sugar

Zope, S. A., & Zope, R. A. (2013, January). Sudarshan kriya yoga: Breathing for health. Retrieved from https://www.ncbi.nlm.nih.gov/pmc/articles/PMC3573542/#:~:text=Neurophysiological model of vagus nerve stimulation pathways&text=To summarize, improved autonomic function, amygdala, and stria terminalis.

The Vagus Nerve and the Healing Promise of The Sudarshan Kriya. (n.d.). Retrieved from https://www.artofliving.org/us-en/the-vagus-nerve-and-the-healing-promise-of-Sudarshan-Kriya

Harvard Health Publishing. (n.d.). The gut-brain connection. Retrieved from https://www.health.harvard.edu/diseases-and-conditions/the-gut-brain-connection

Levac, K. A. (n.d.). Research on Diaphragmatic Breathing. Retrieved from https://www.nqa.org/index.php?option=com_dailyplanetblog&view=entry&year=2019&month=07&day=01&id=35:research-on-diaphragmatic-breathing

www.ingramcontent.com/pod-product-compliance
Lightning Source LLC
Chambersburg PA
CBHW050312120526
44592CB00014B/1873